# Krampus The "Koloring" Book

## Vol. 2 Horrid Coloring books

By

Jordan R. Colton

Introduction by

Christian J. Colton

# DEDICATION

This is dedicated to my growing fans of this little Horrid Coloring Book company. We are over 2000+ strong so far and slowly we are growing more and more! Thanks everyone!

# ACKNOWLEDGMENTS

I wish to acknowledge my family in supporting me in this next volume. They helped me to keep going and to realize that I couldn't go the quick easy route because I have set a standard for Horror coloring books and I shouldn't deter from that. Thanks for your honest criticism and thoughts and opinions.

Also thank you for the archivers and collaborators who had the vintage images of Krampus that I was able to use for inspiration for this coloring book! If it wasn't for your work this book would not be possible!

Jordan Colton Presents

A Horrid Coloring Book

# <u>Krampus</u> The "Koloring" Book

# Introduction

The Krampus. We may have forgotten this demonic companion of St. Nickolaus for a time, but it is clear we need him now more than ever. The Krampus would accompany St. Nickolaus as they judged the hopeful little boys and girls at Christmas Time. If the children were good, from his sack St. Nickolaus would give them gifts and sweets. But if the children were bad, St. Nickolaus left them to the Krampus and his punishment.

The Krampus's name comes from the old Norse word for *claw*. The Krampus is covered in black fur, horns upon his head with cloven hooves for feet. His teeth are sharp. The thorny switch he wields stings the skin of naughty children everywhere. His long tongue then licks up the children's tears. In his basket, the Krampus stuffs the naughty children to take them to his lair, perhaps hell itself. There he whips them. There he cooks them. And there he eats them.

It's no surprise this ancient yuletide terror is making a comeback. The modern celebration of Christmas does its' best to make us forget how awful we can be. With its' shiny and bright commercialism, the "Good Tidings We Bring" greeting card schlock, the high-fructose visions of sugar plums dancing along our waistlines, Christmas time hypnotizes us into thinking we can do no wrong, that it's all good. Santa doesn't really check the naughty list, does he?

But the Krampus knows better. We have been naughty little children & the Krampus is here to make us pay!

Happy Holidays, and Happy Coloring!

- Christian J. Colton

    Krampus Historiographer

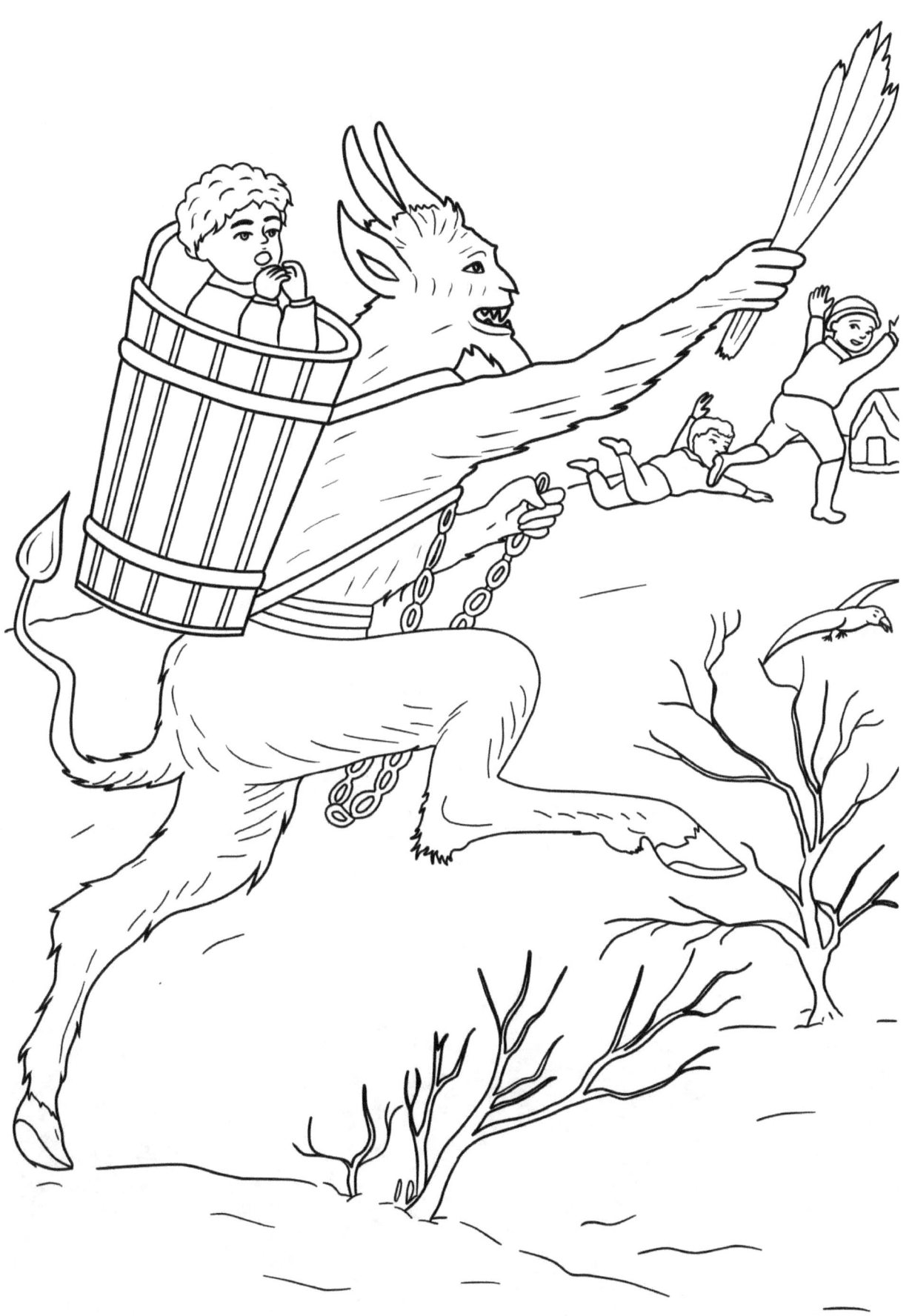

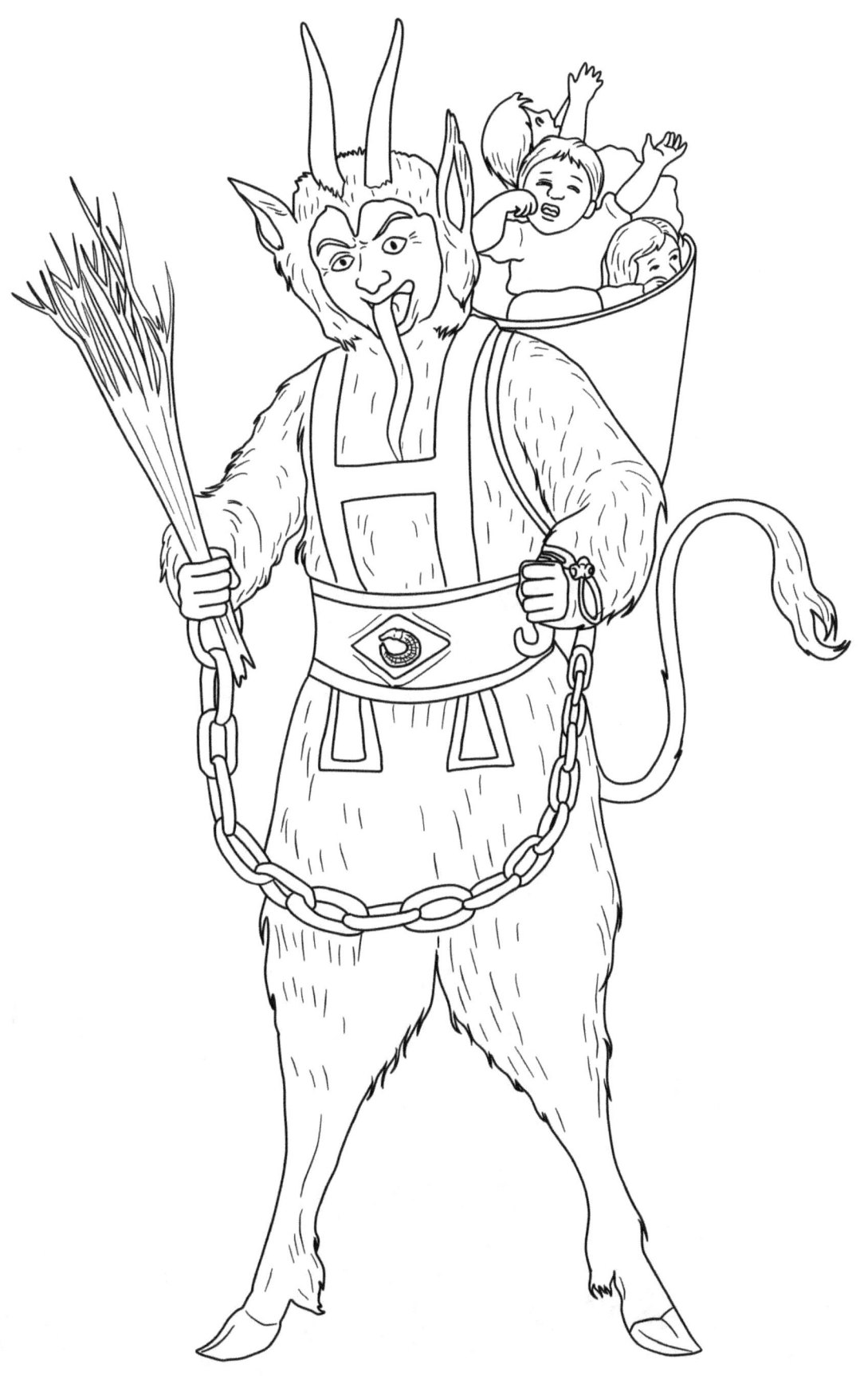

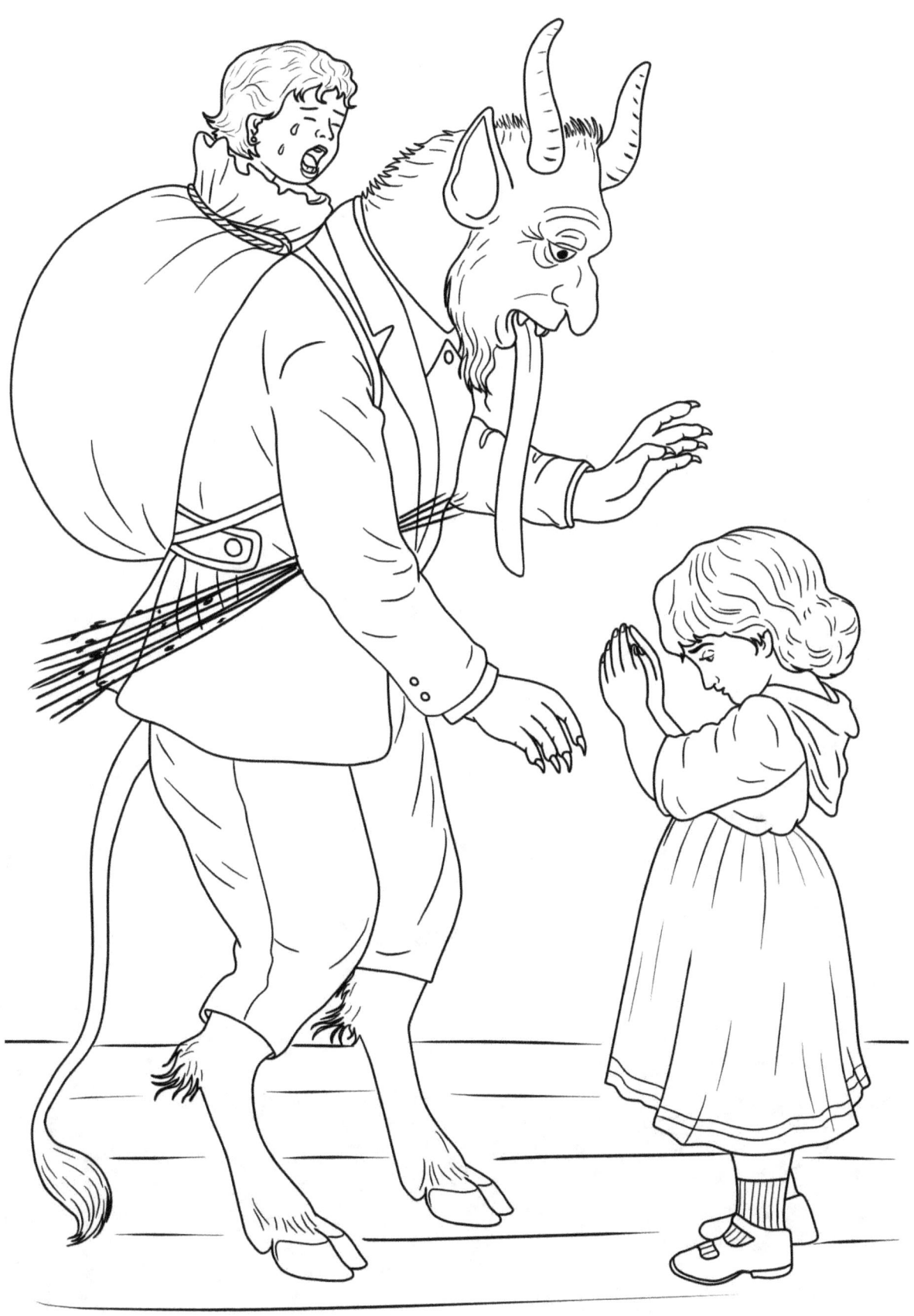

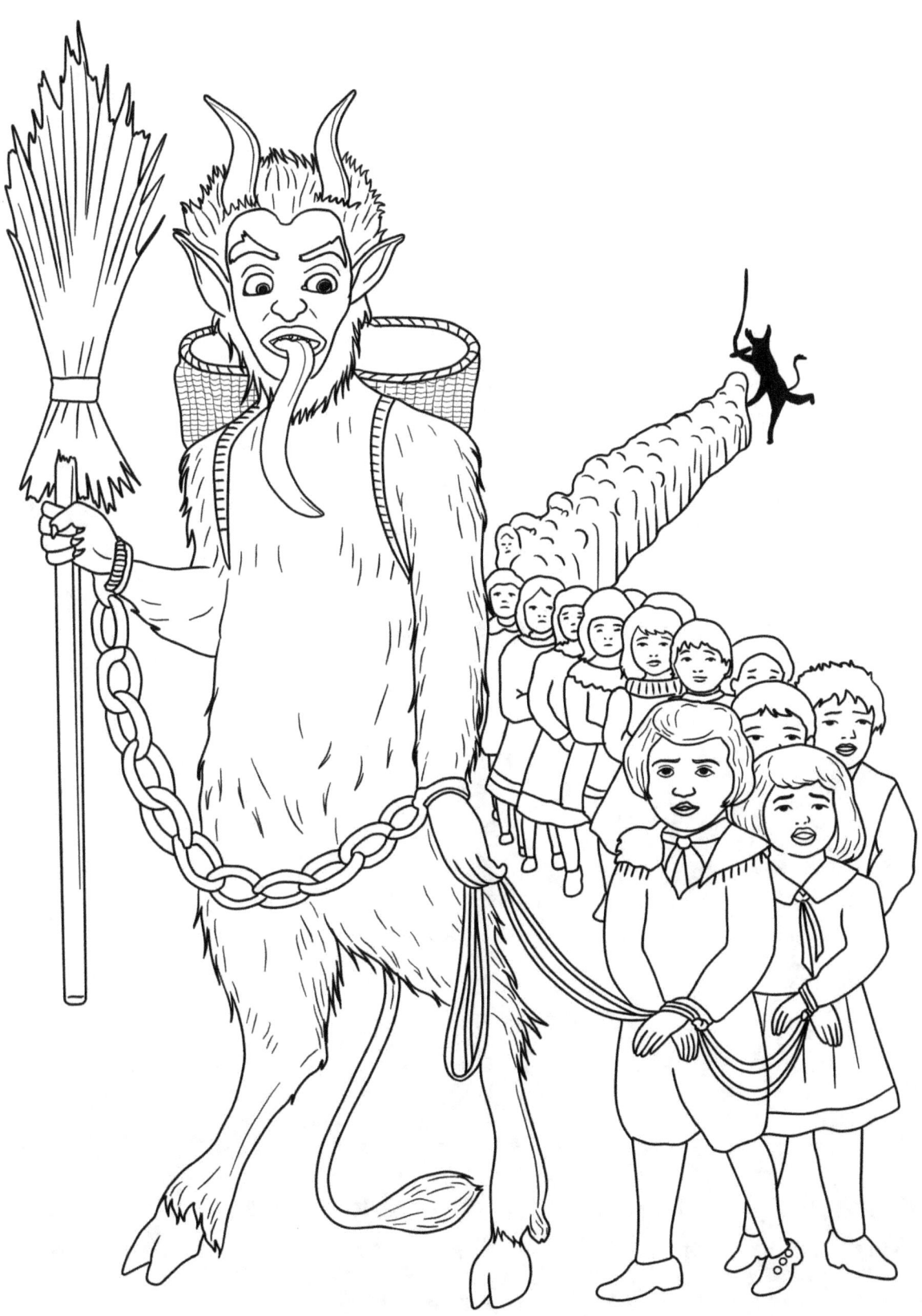

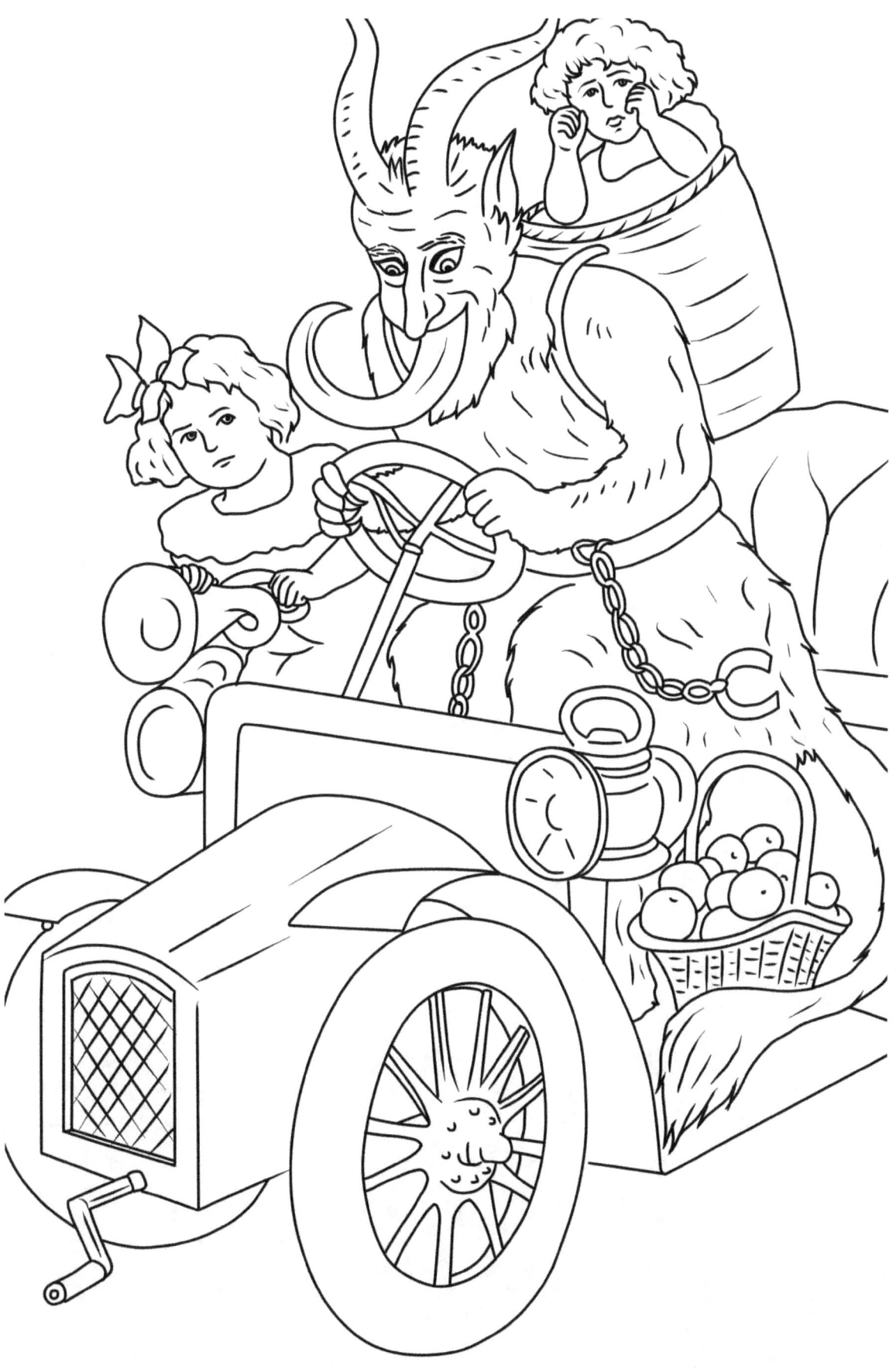

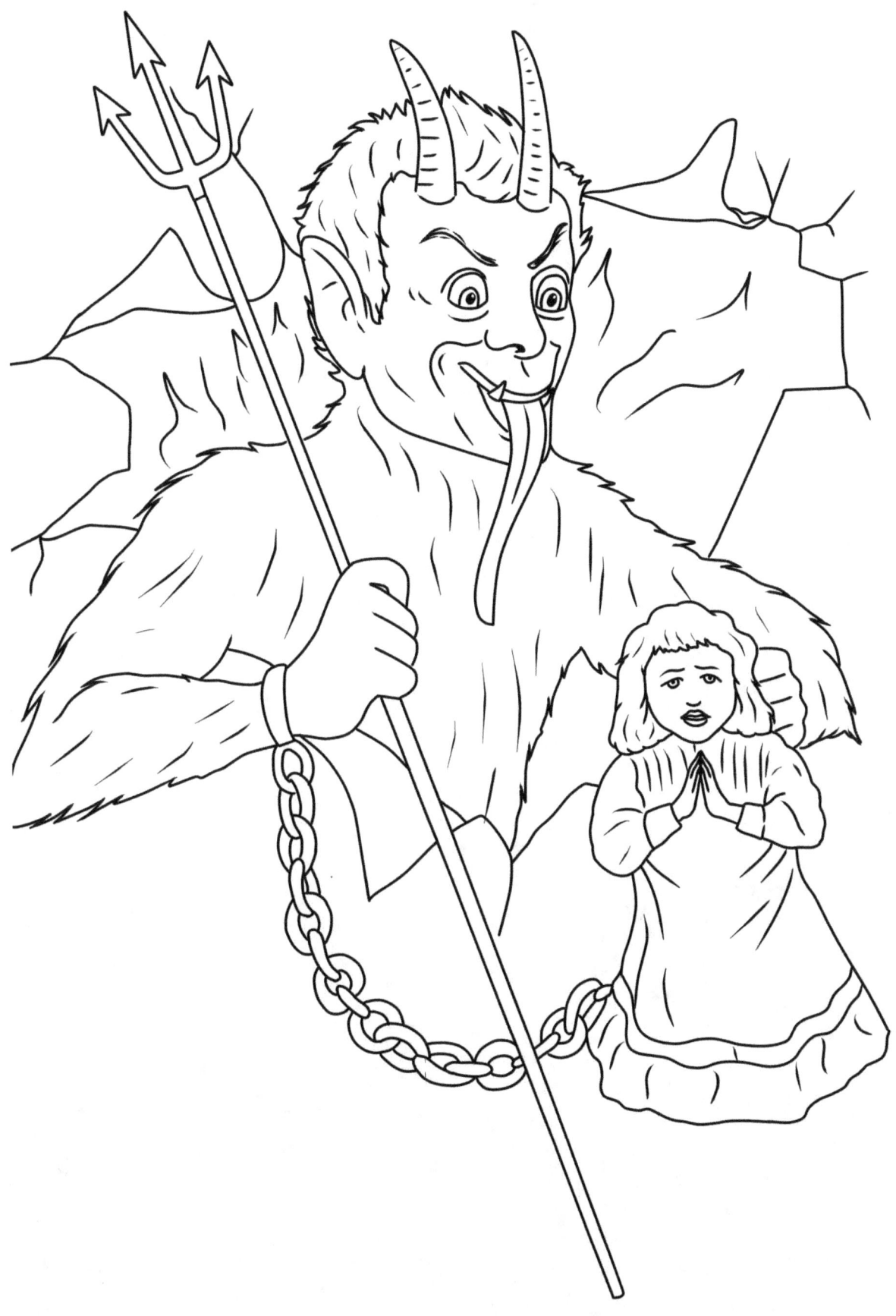

Krampus Koloring Book

Krampus Koloring Book

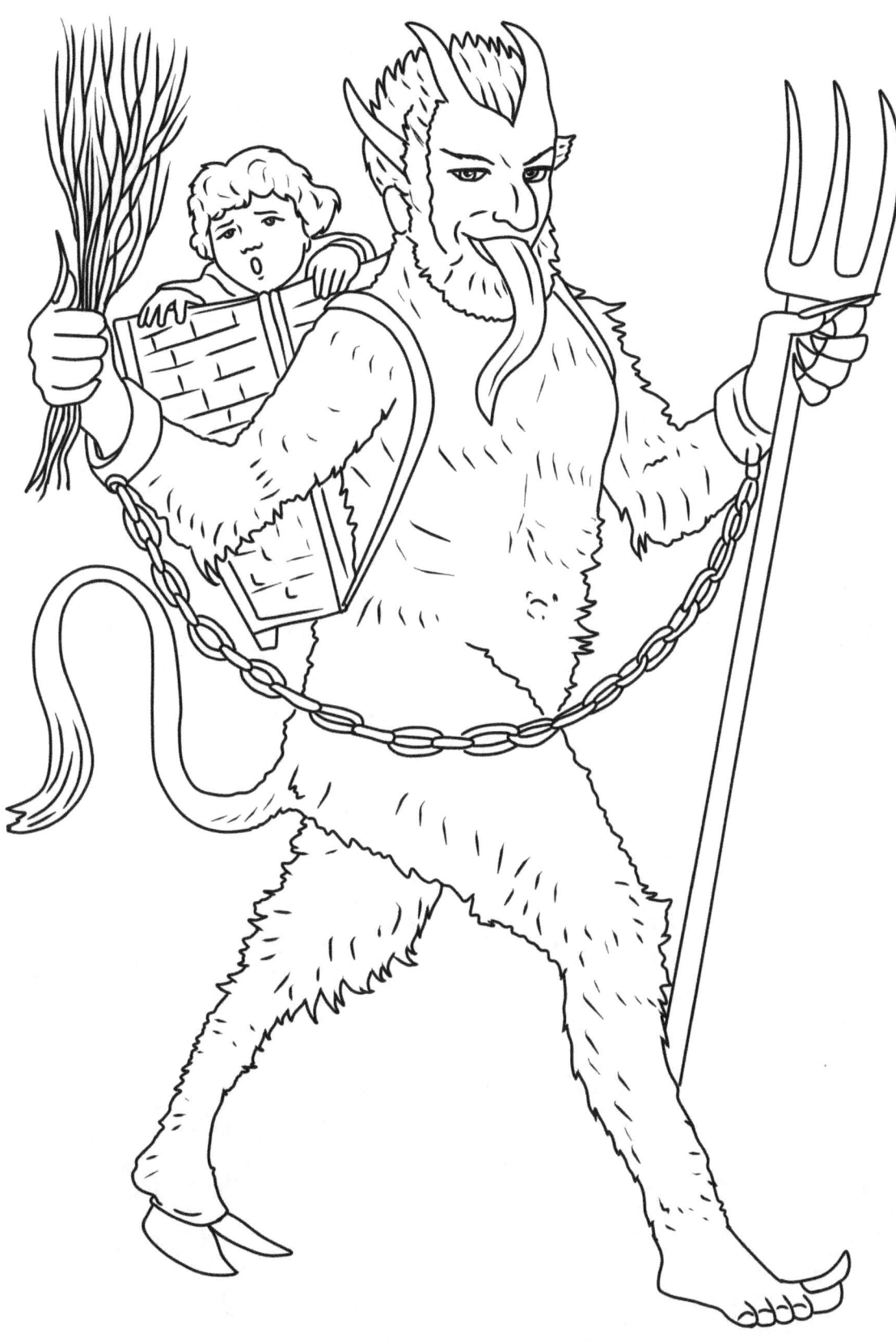

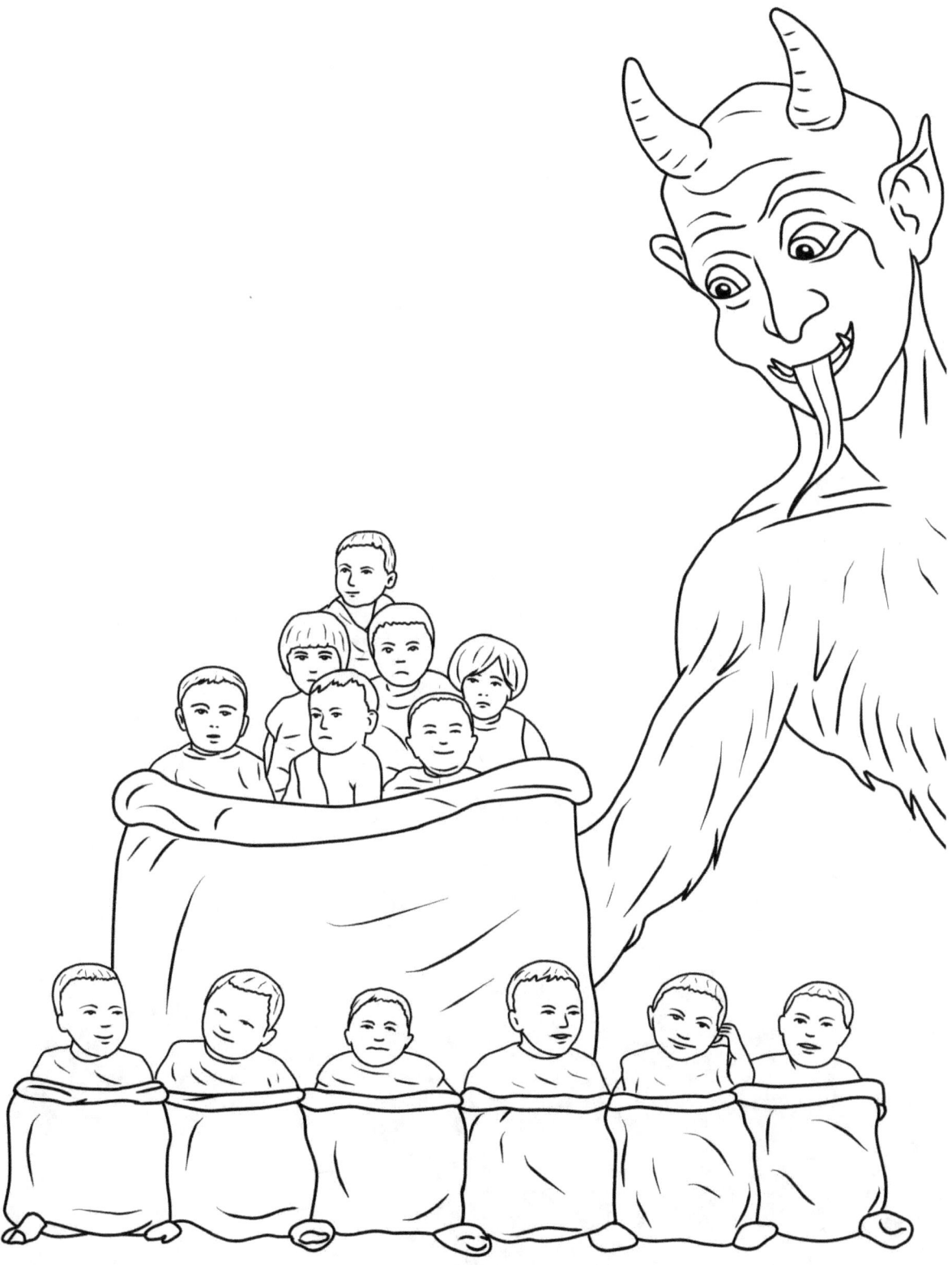

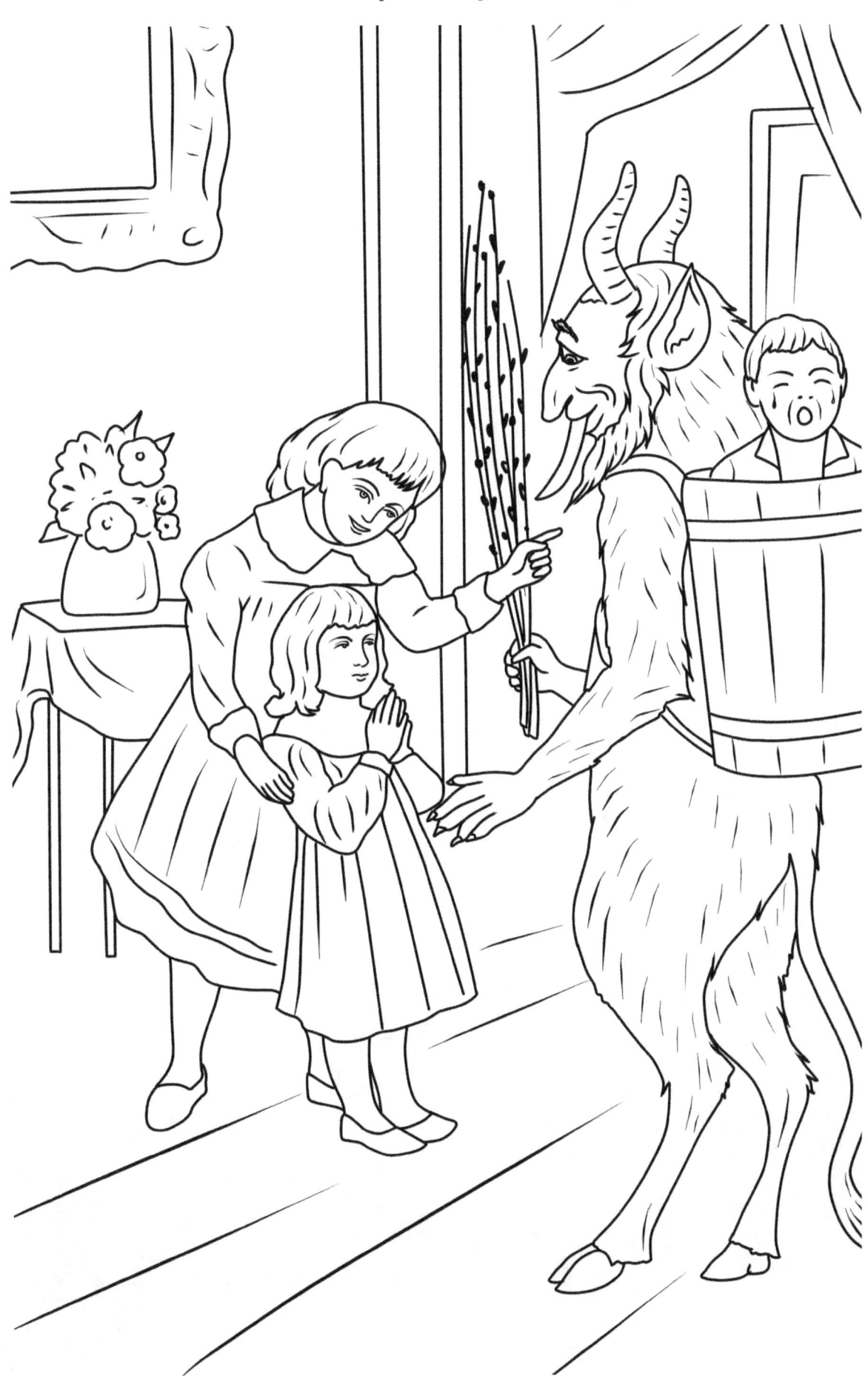

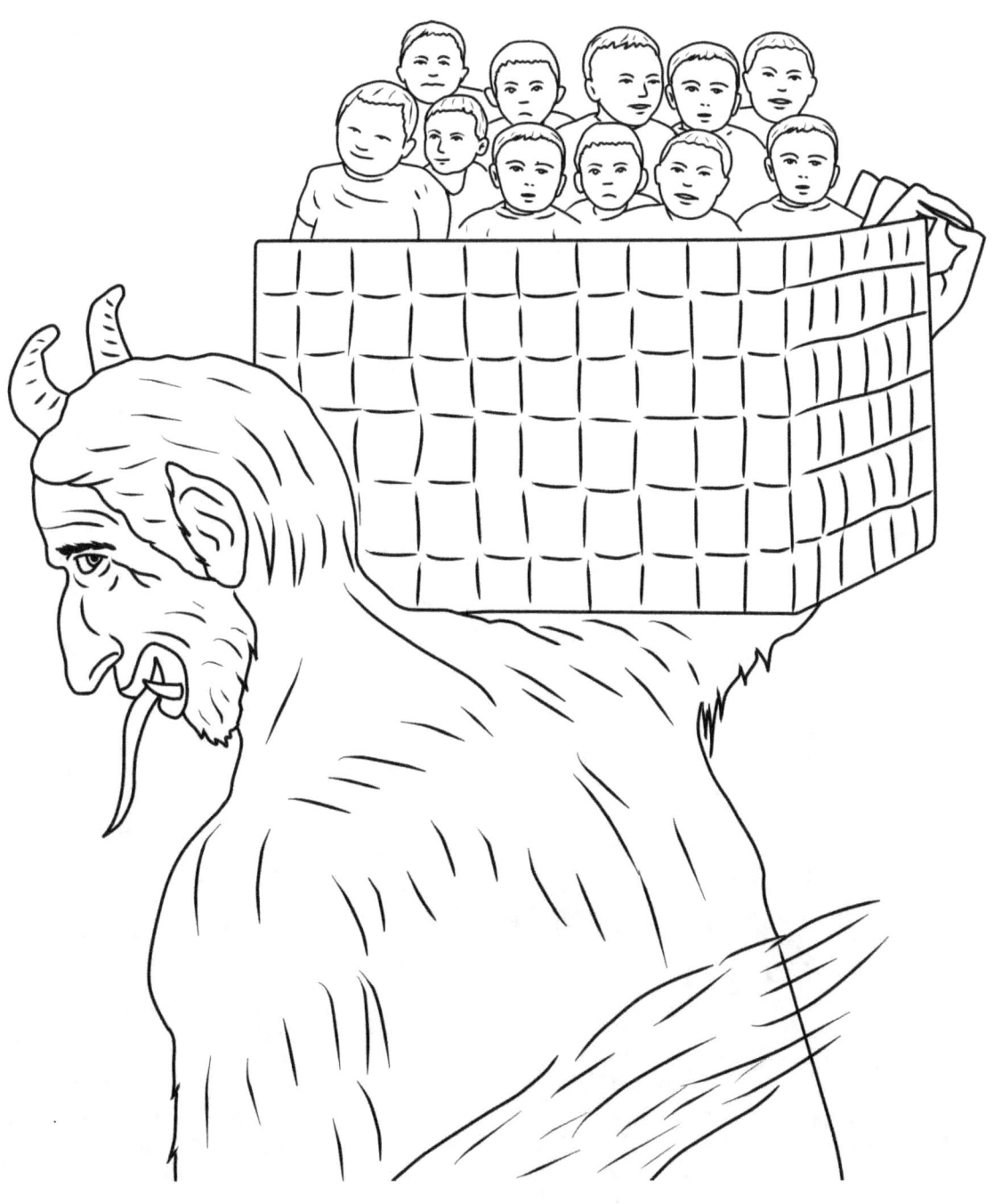

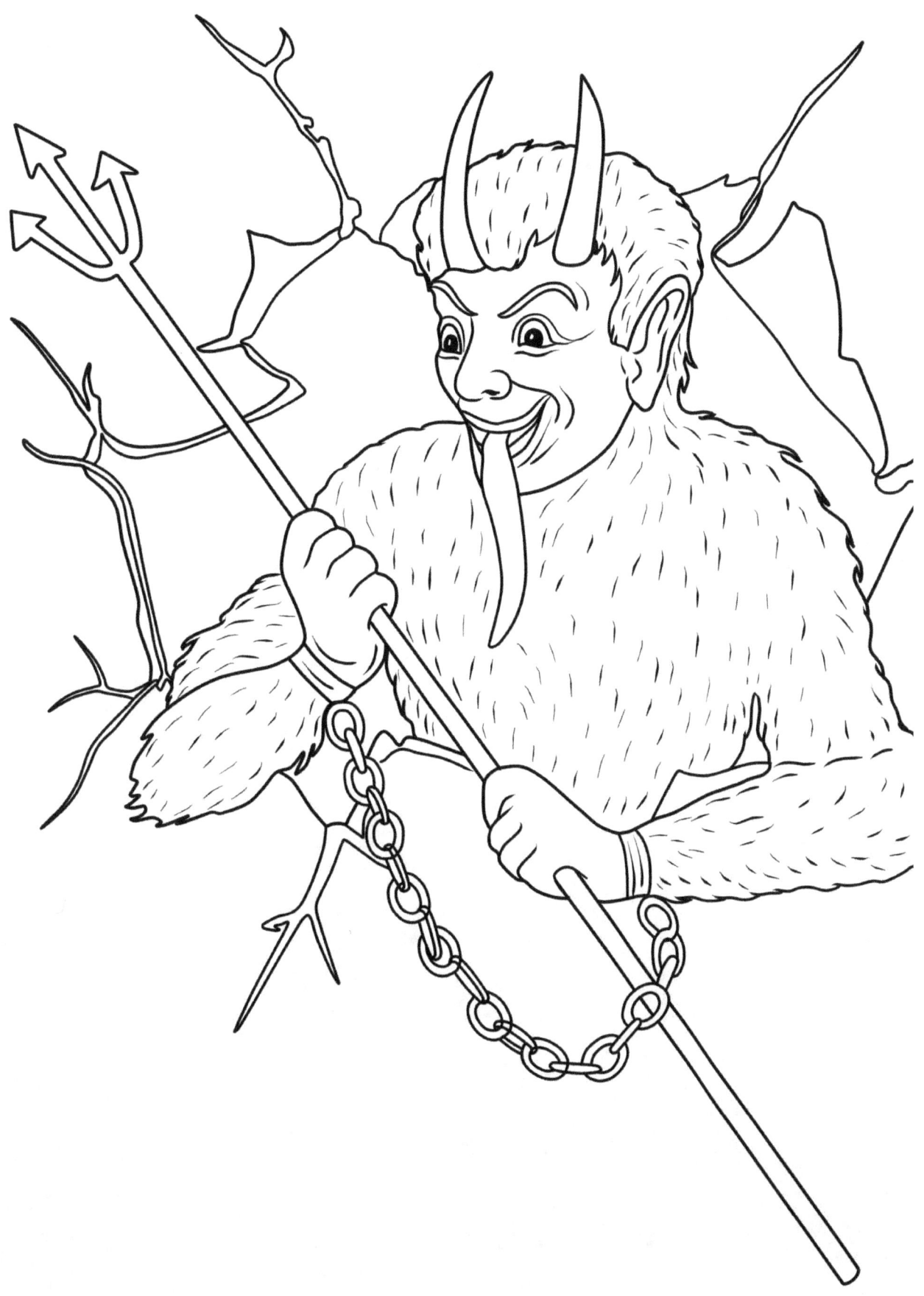

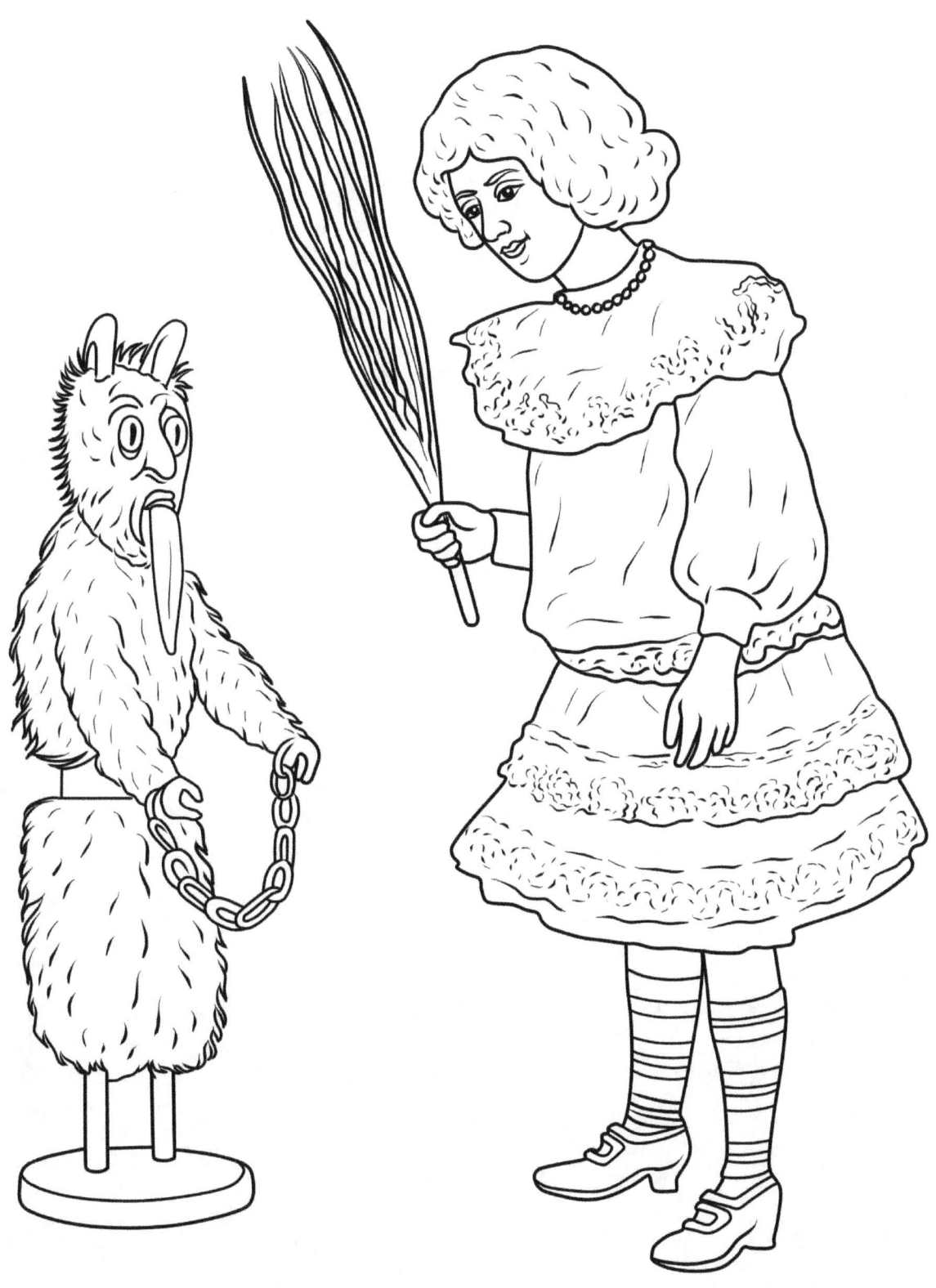

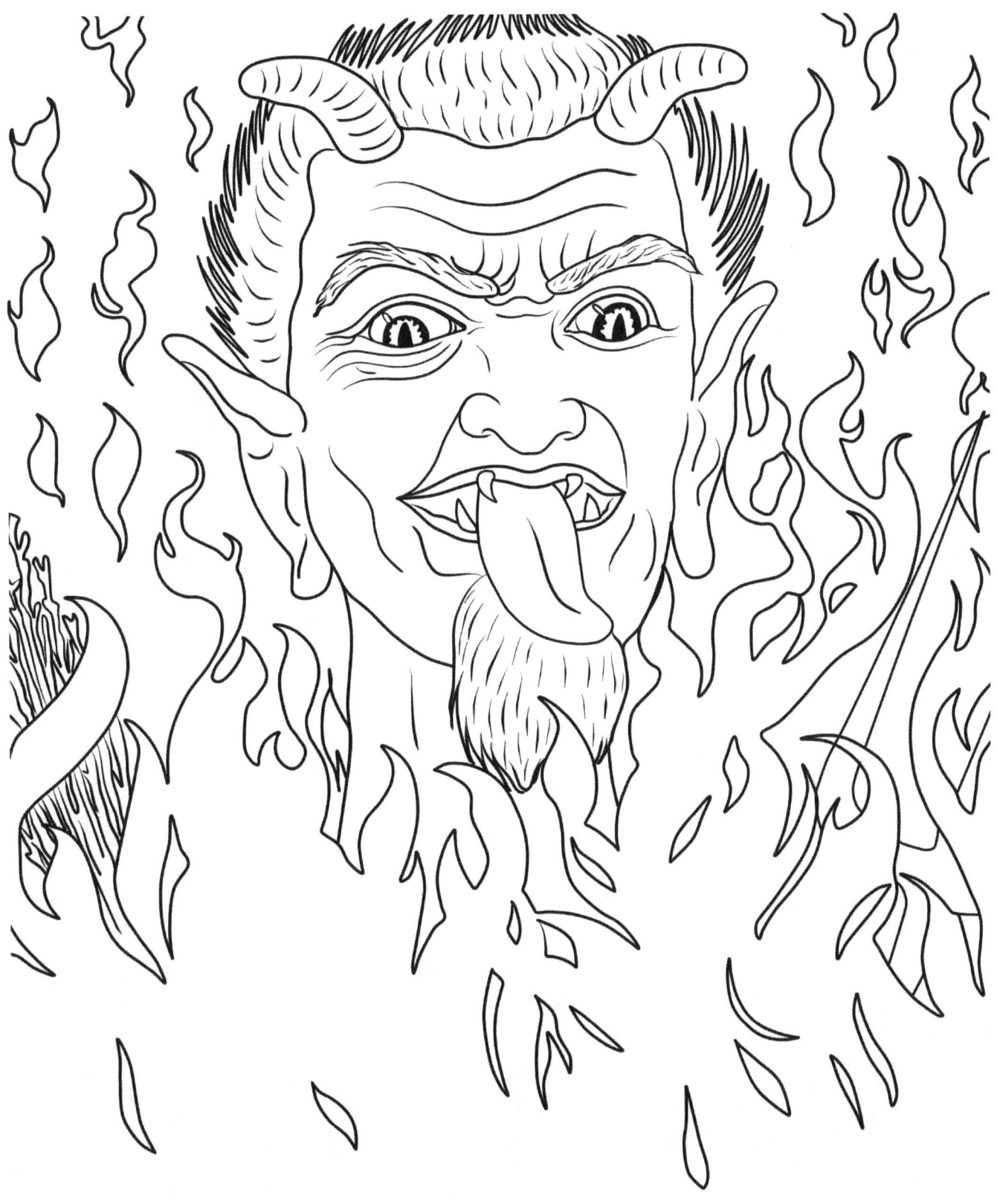

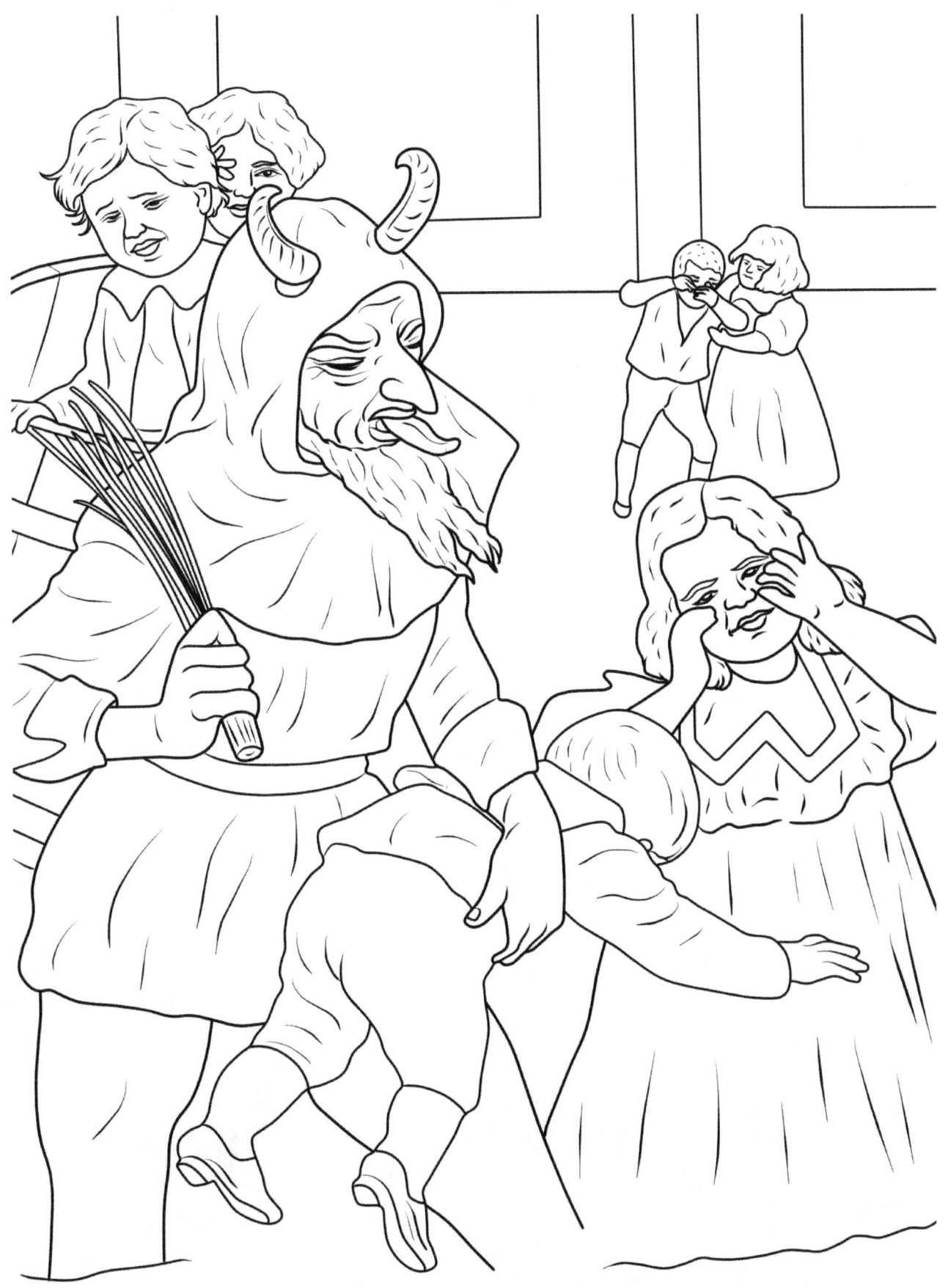

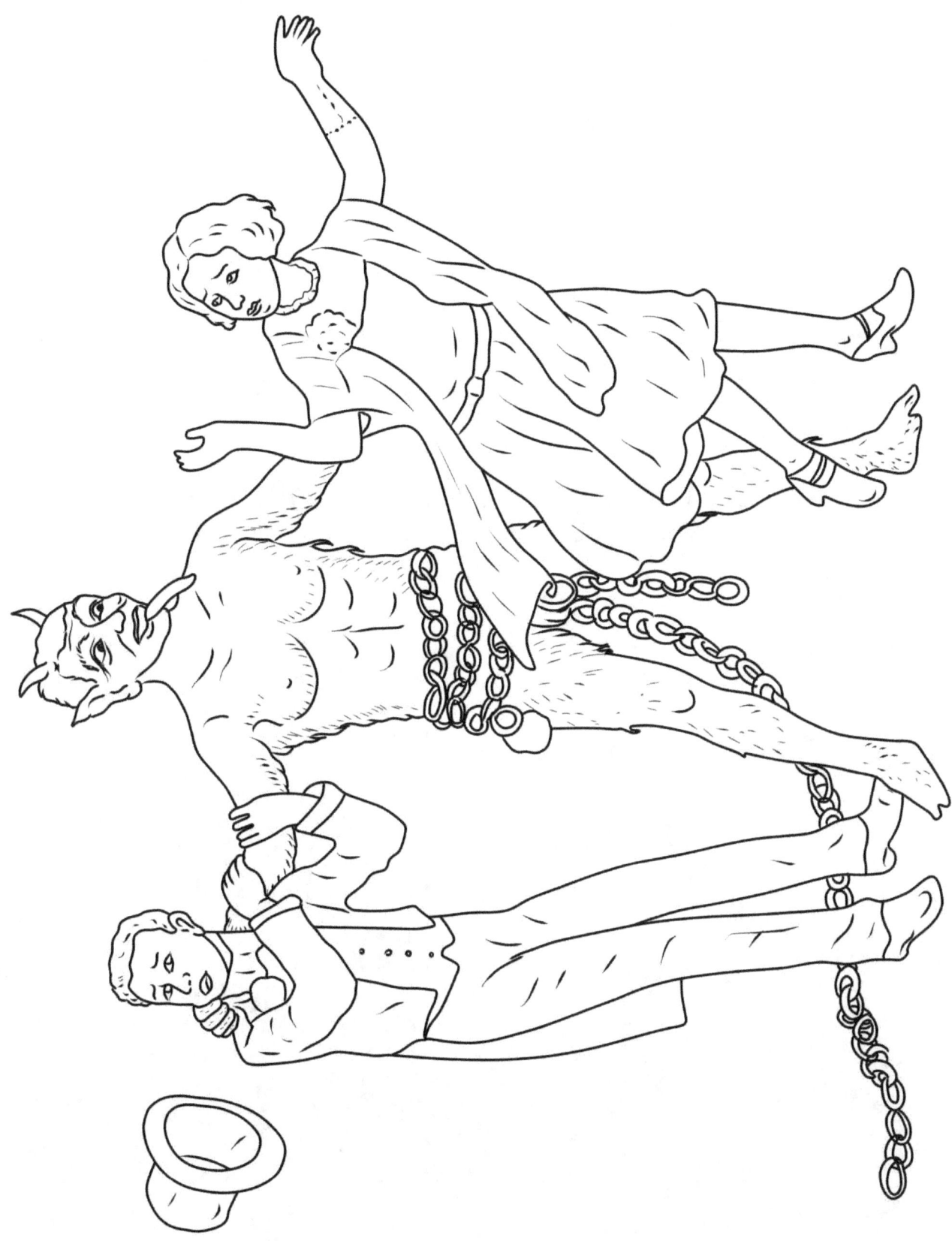

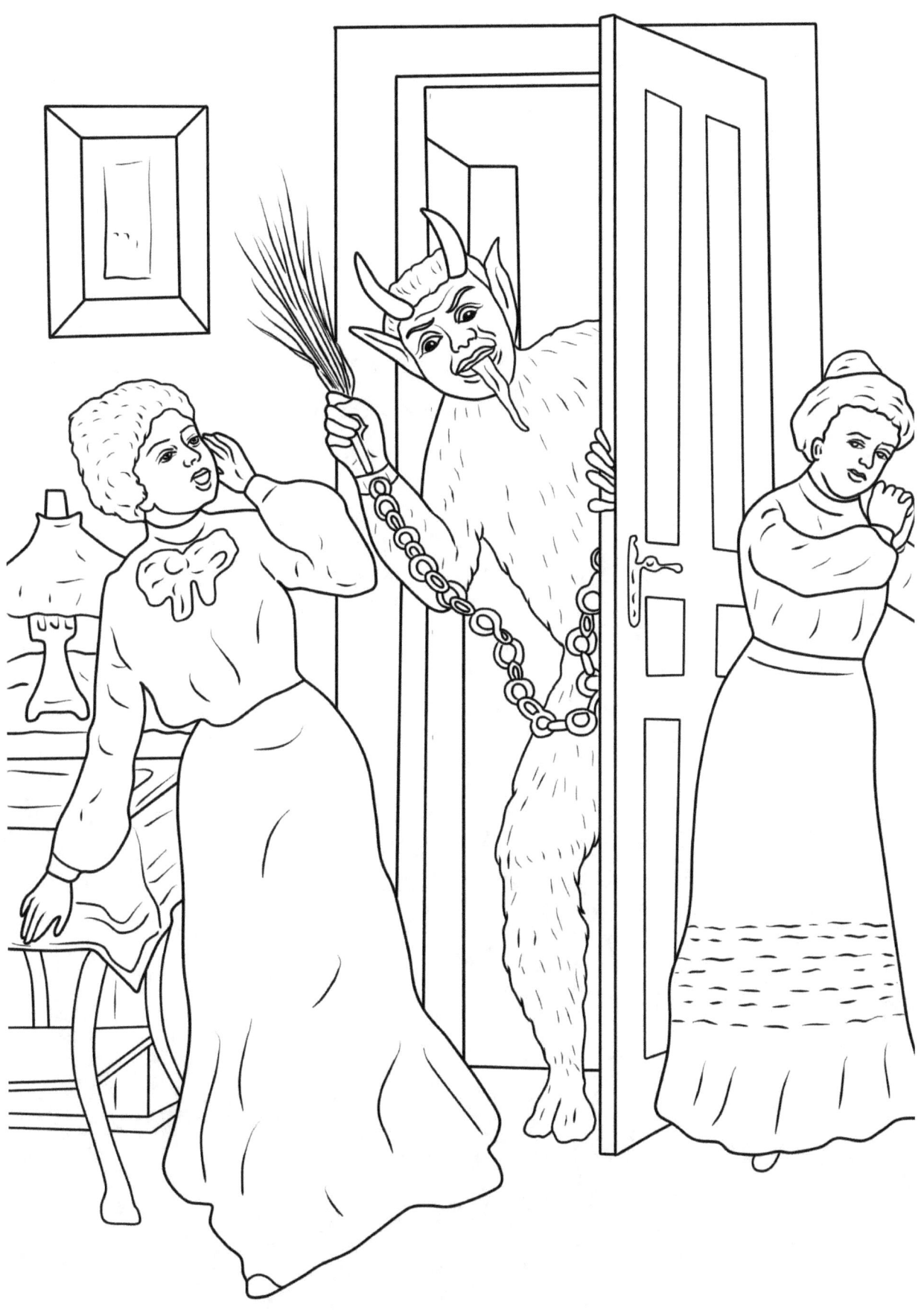

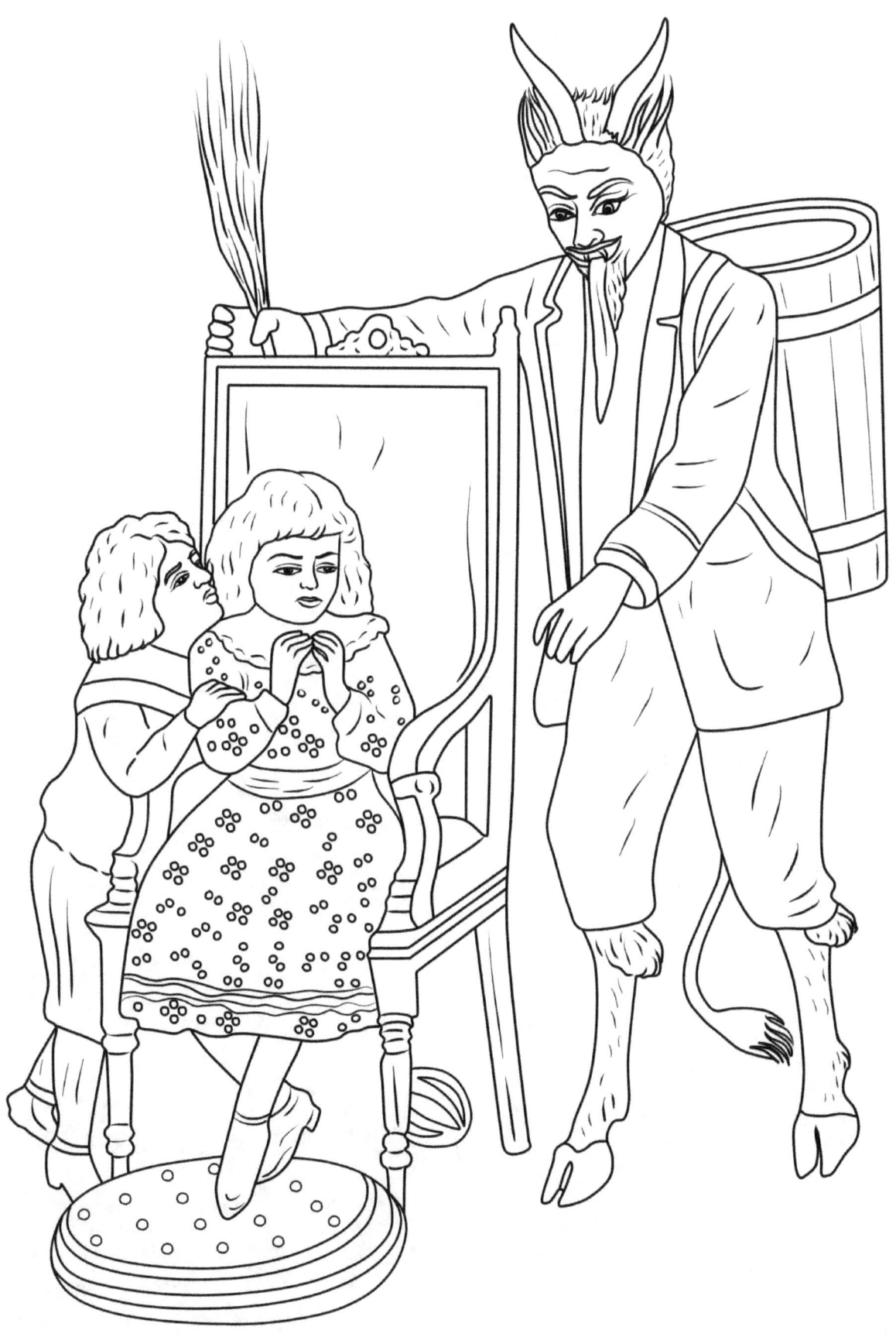

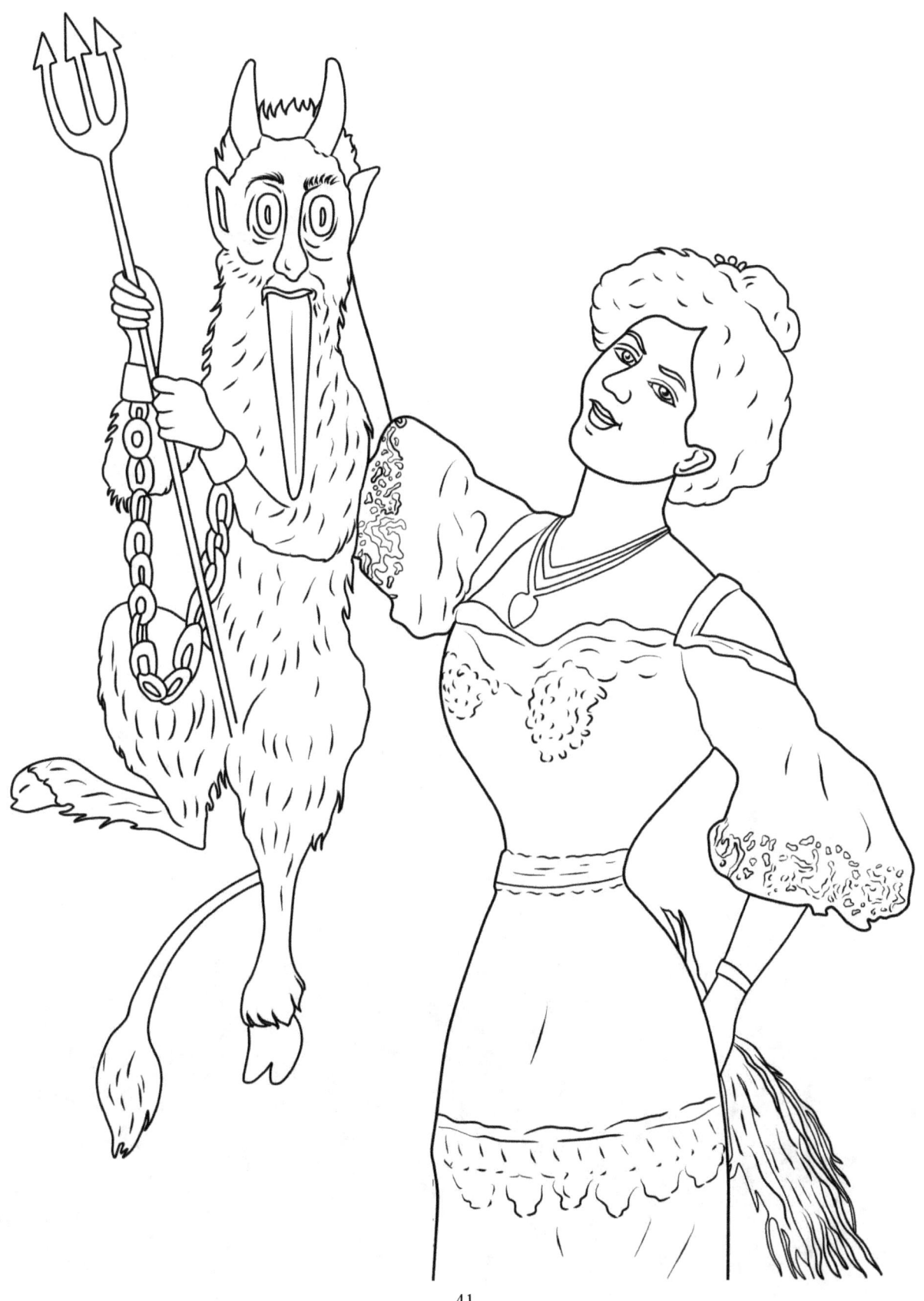

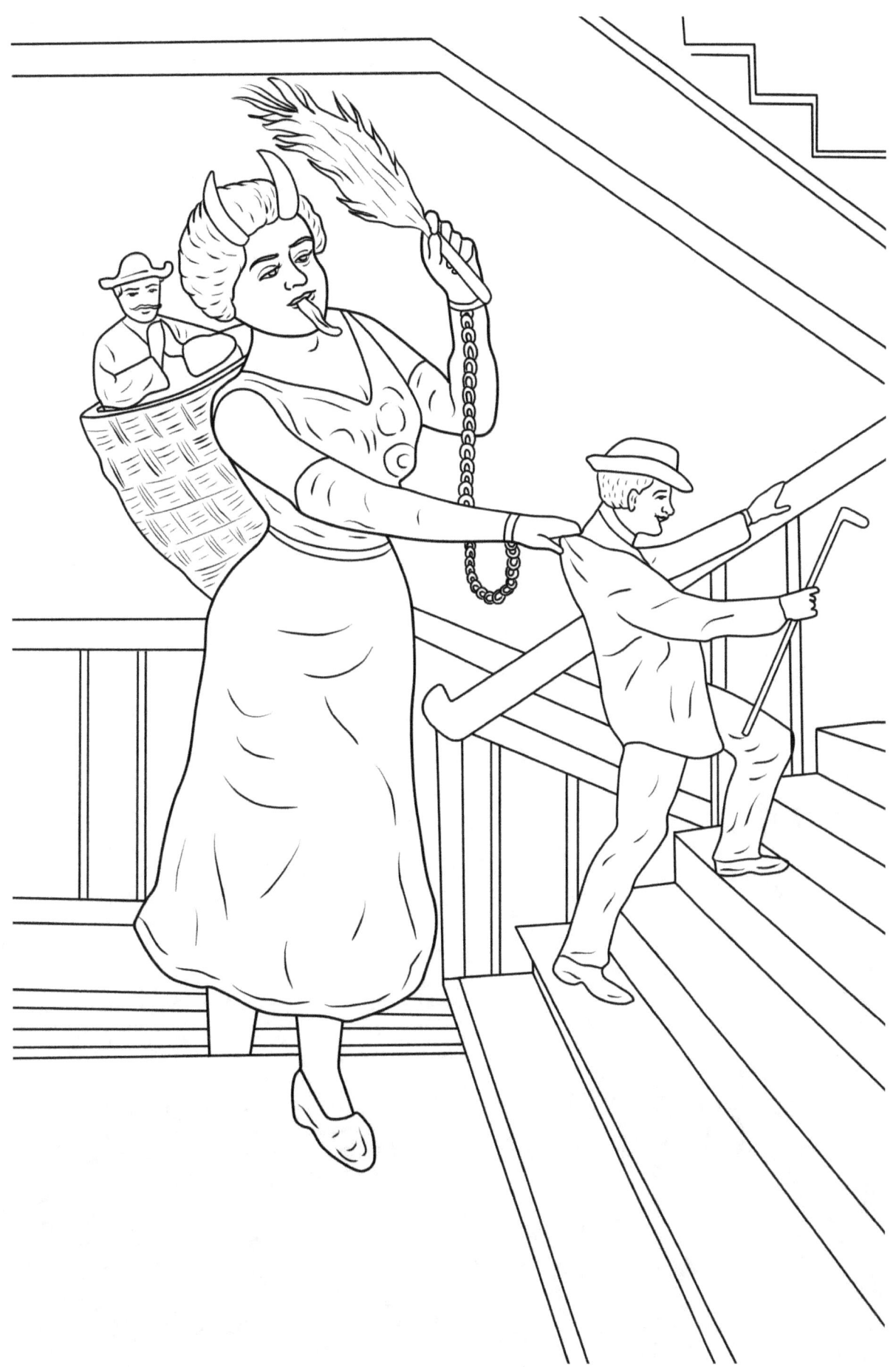

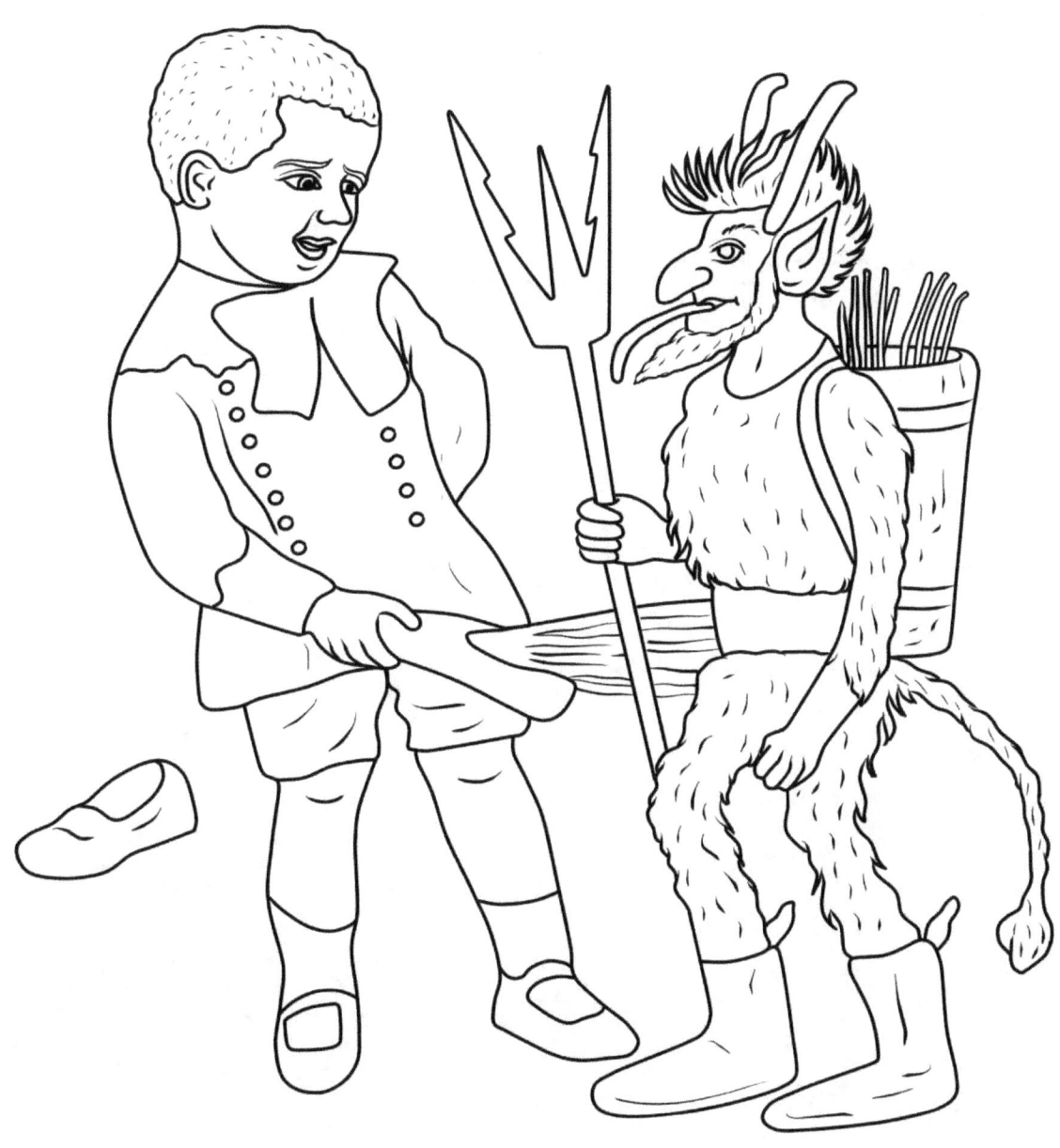

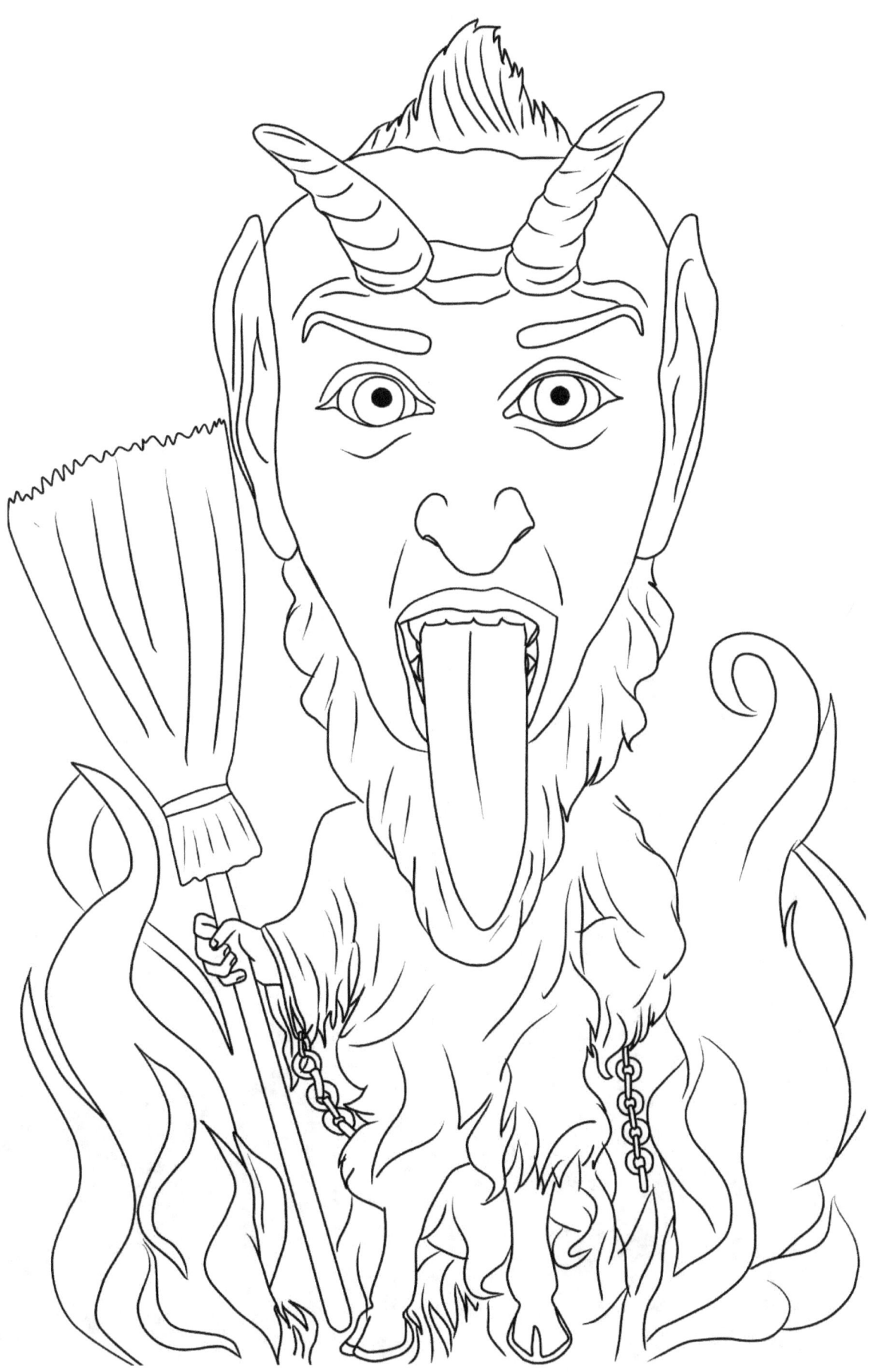

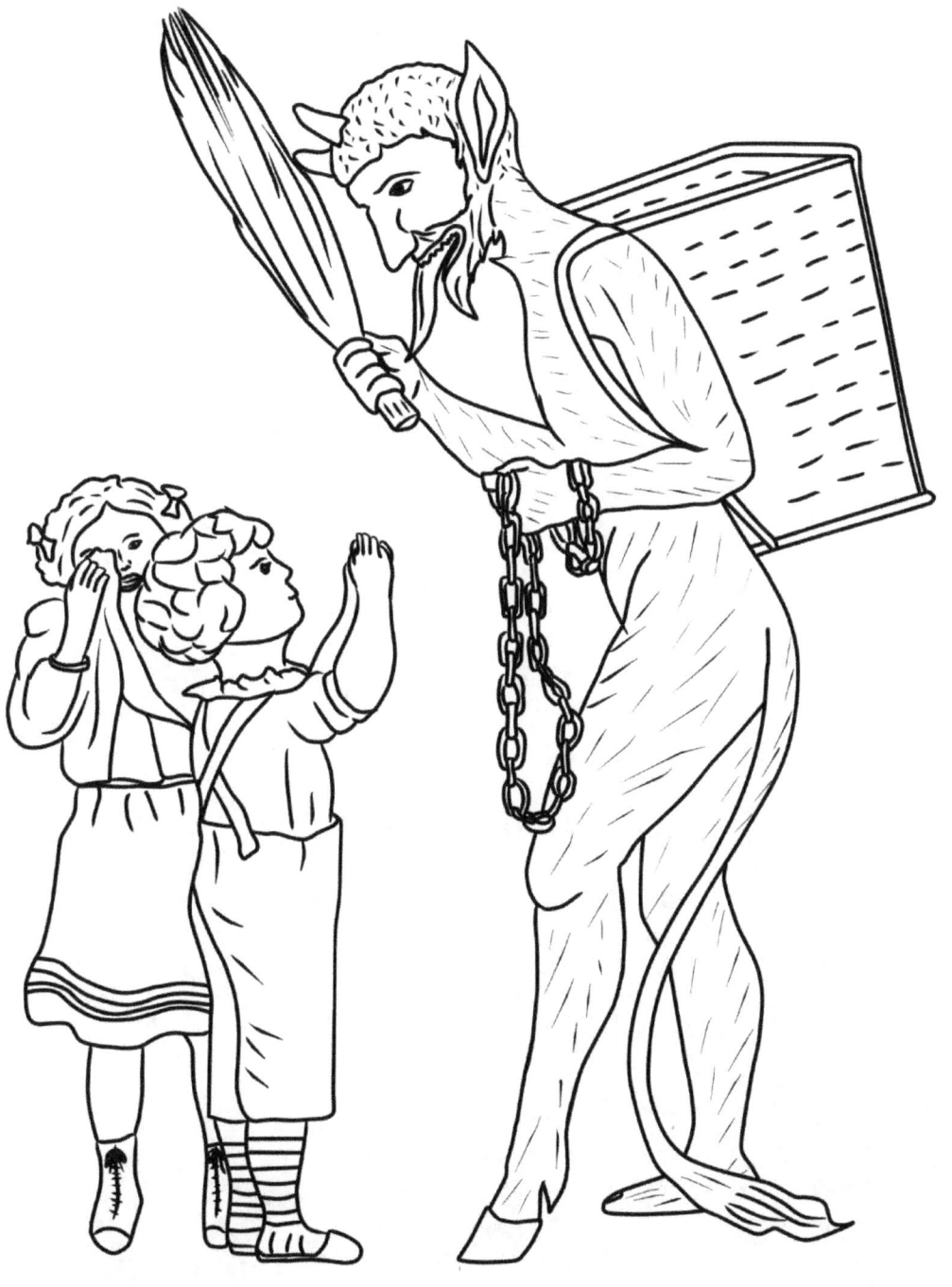

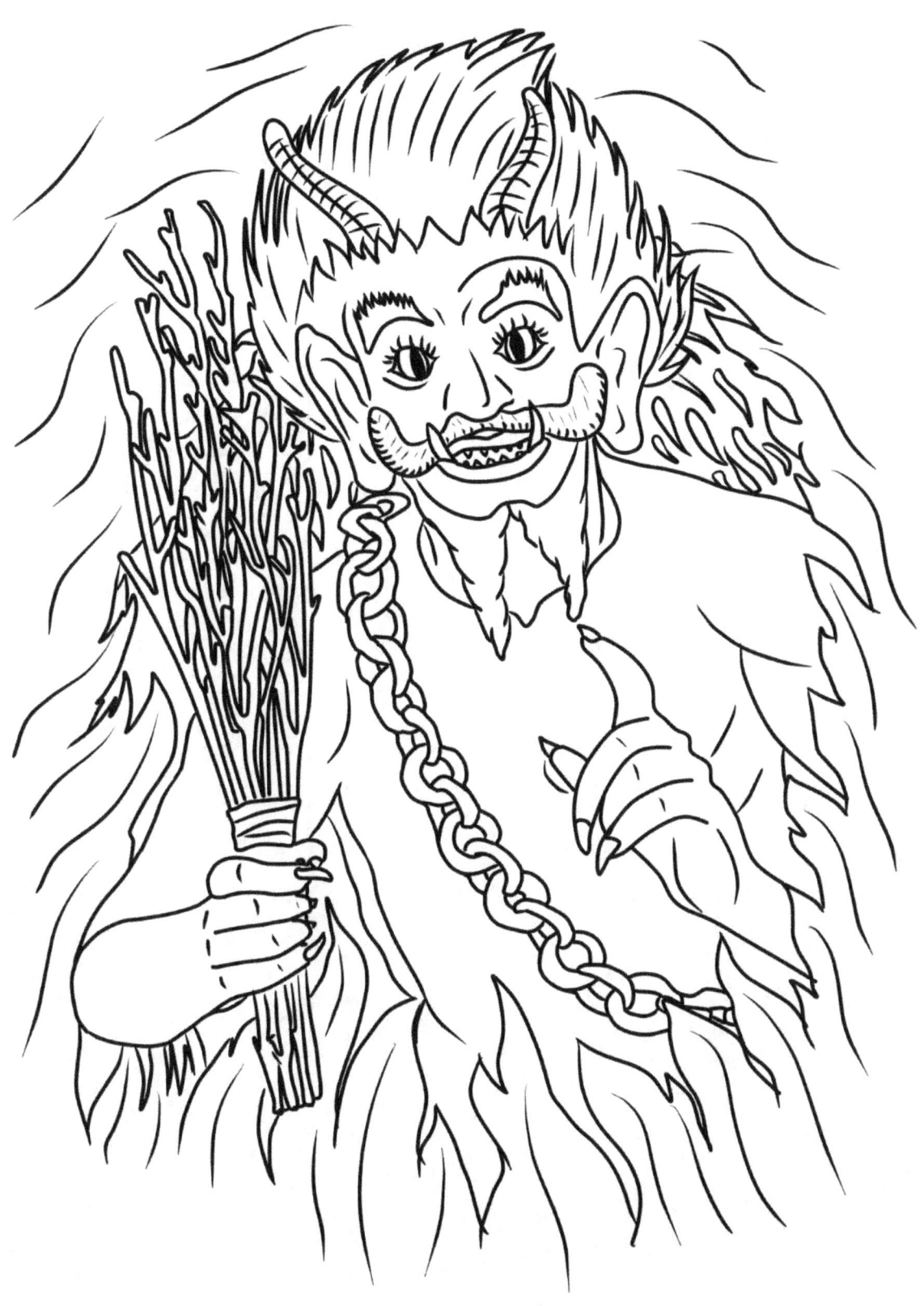

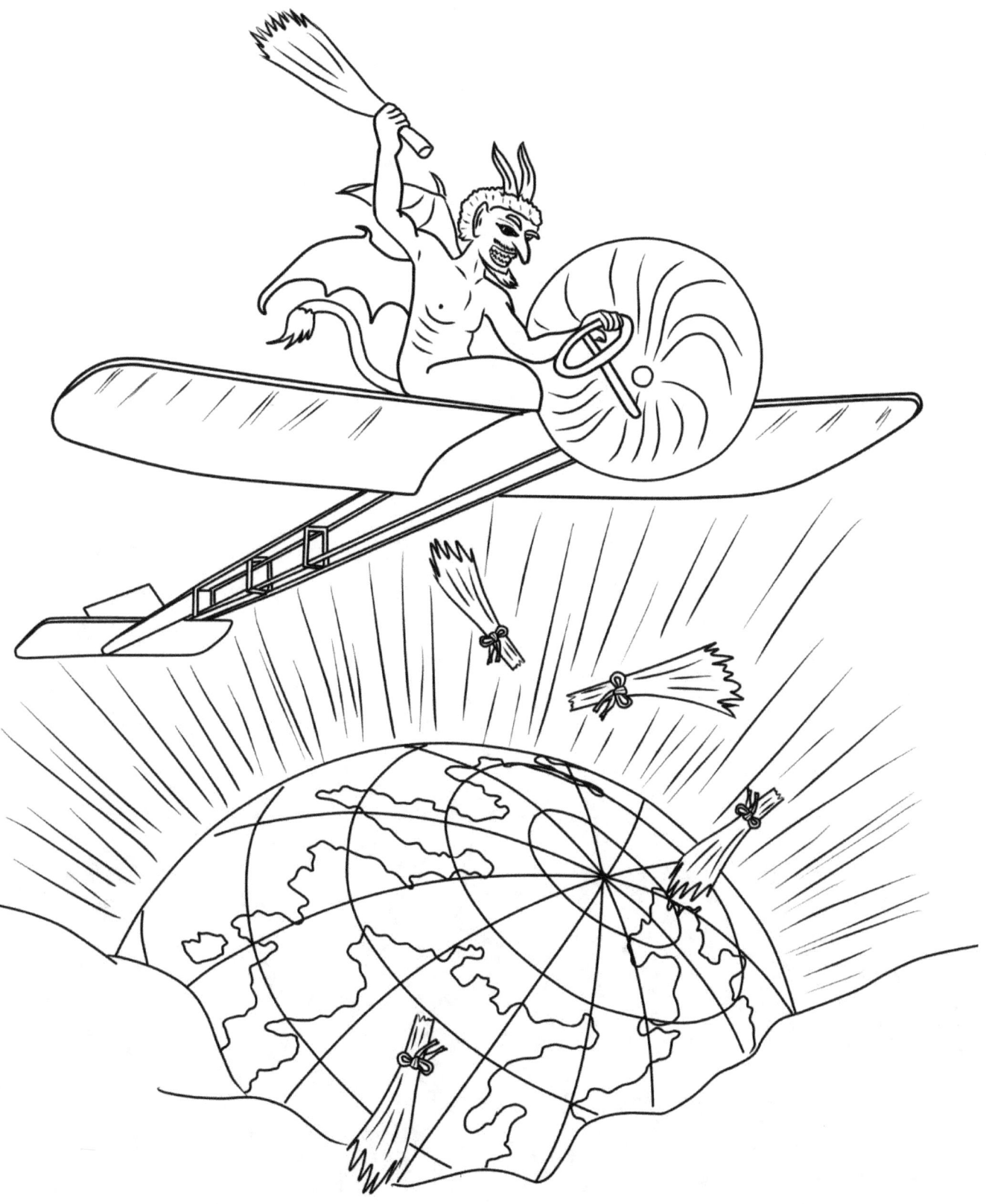

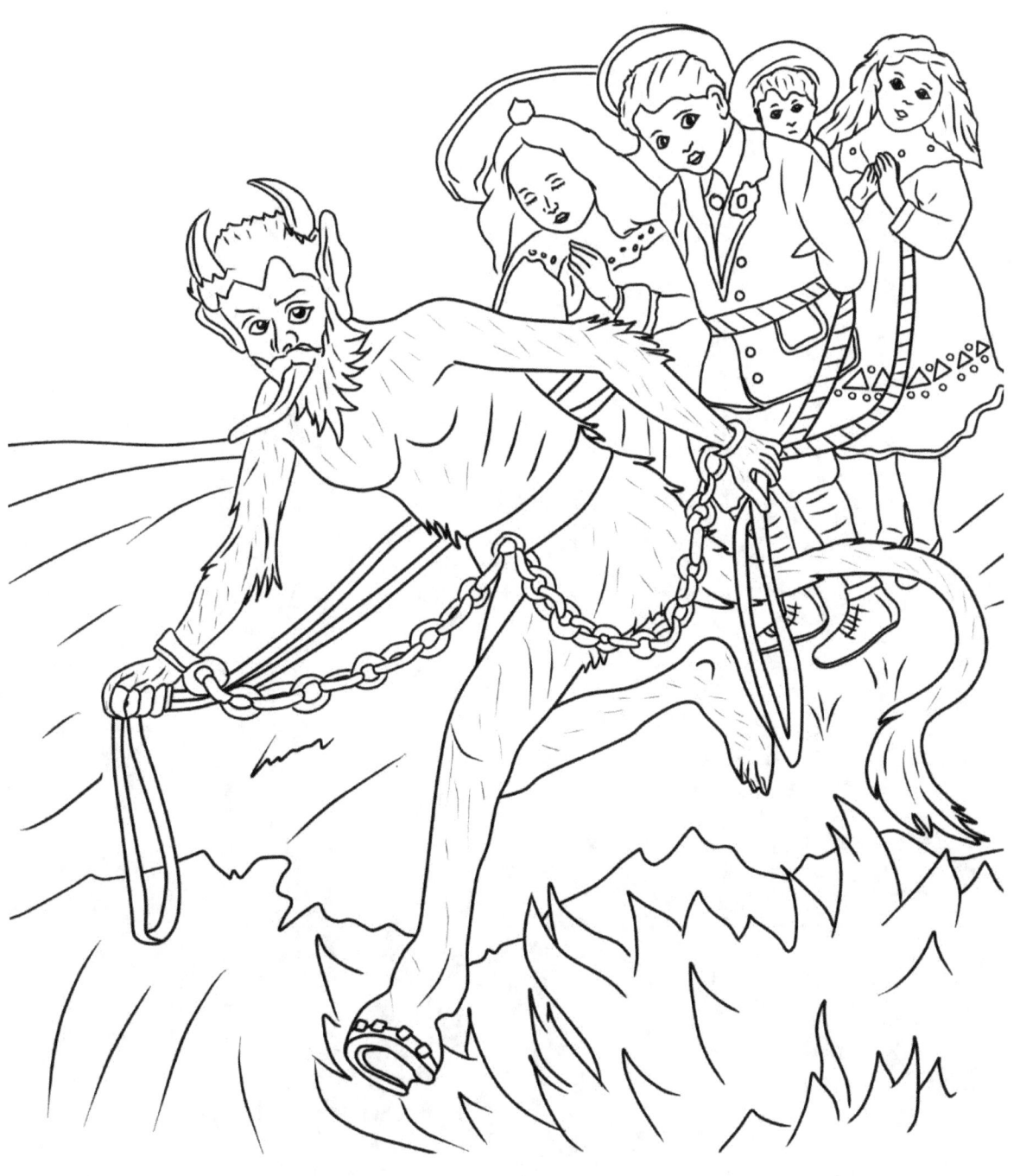

Krampus Koloring Book

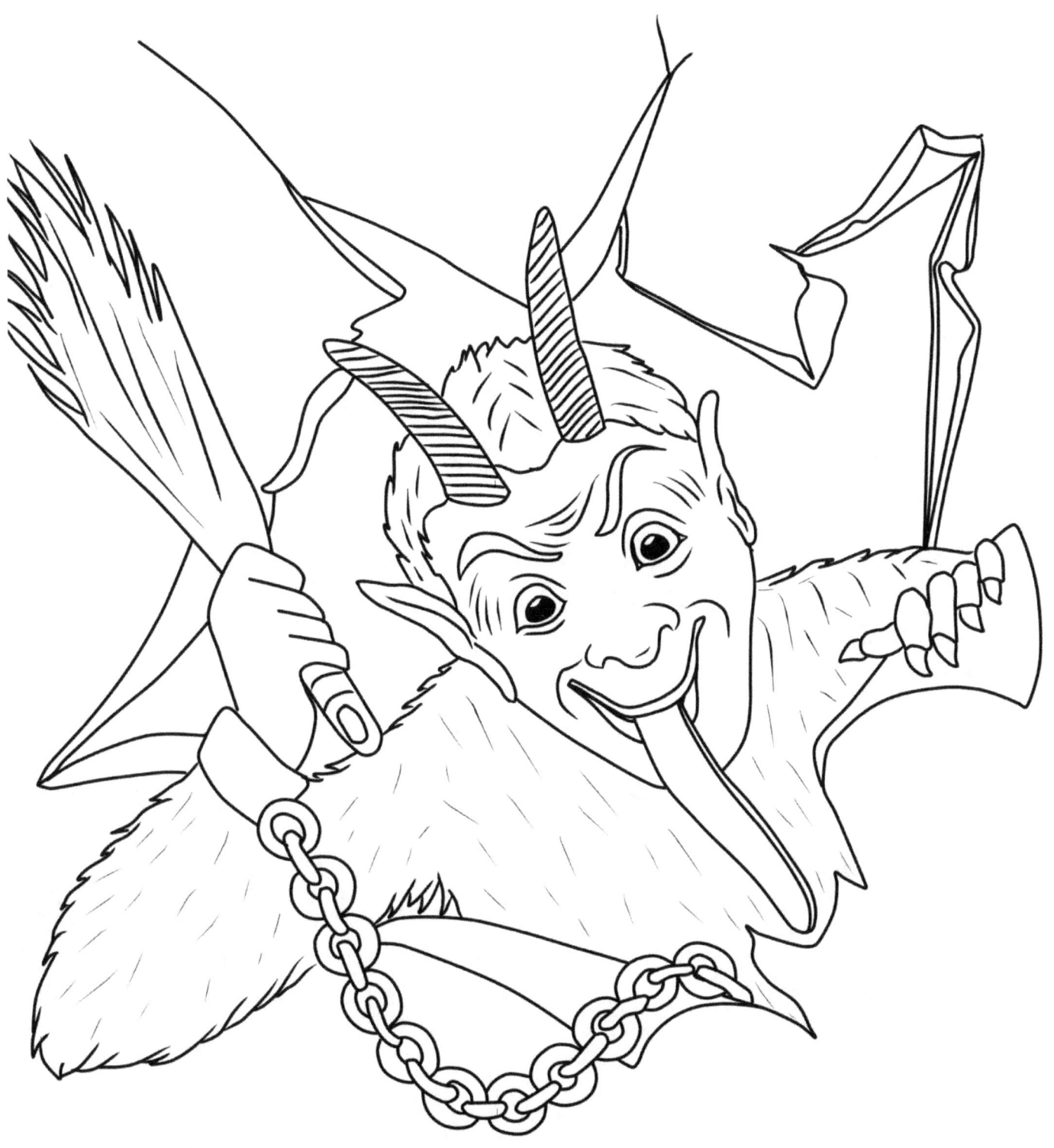

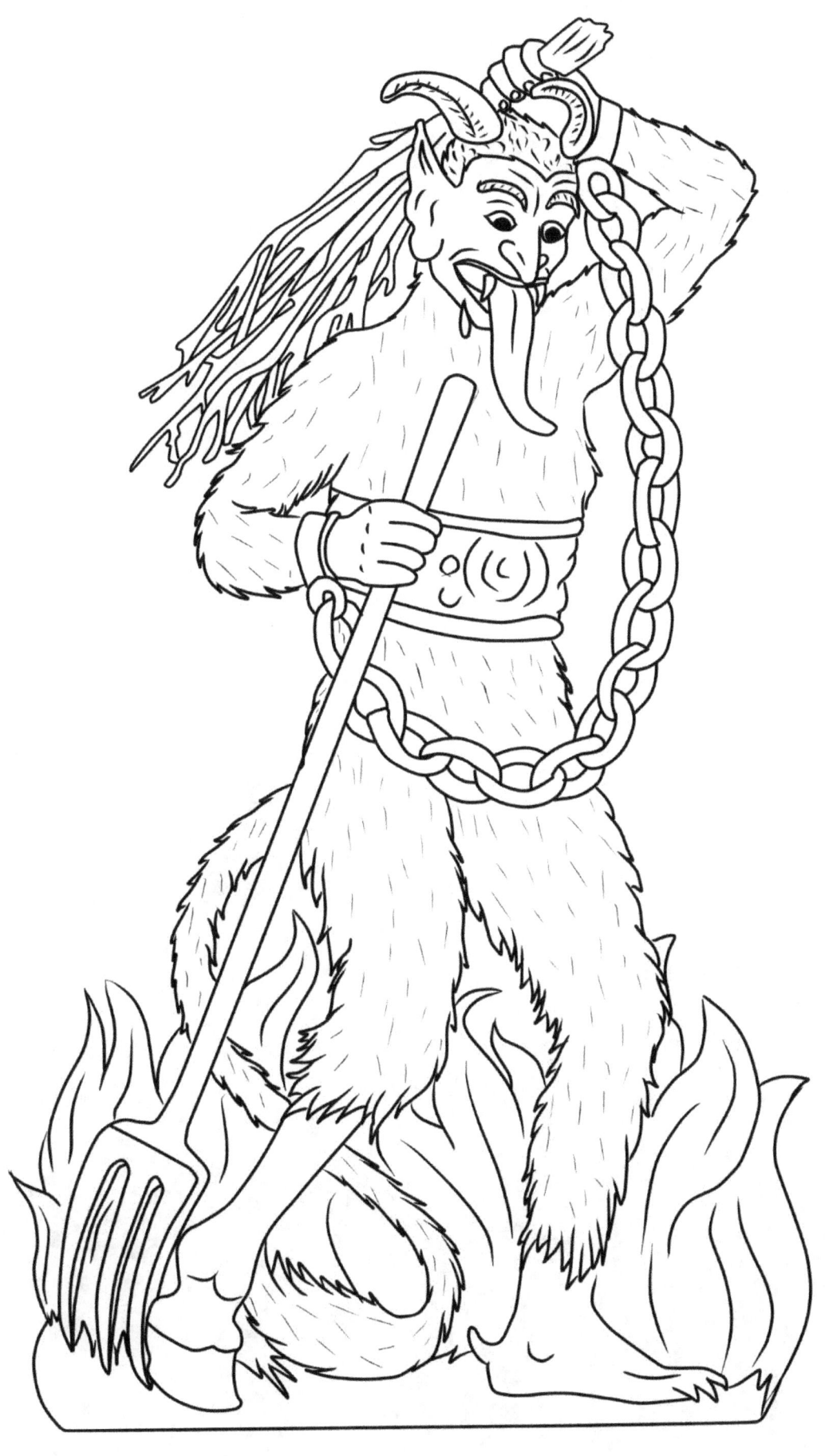

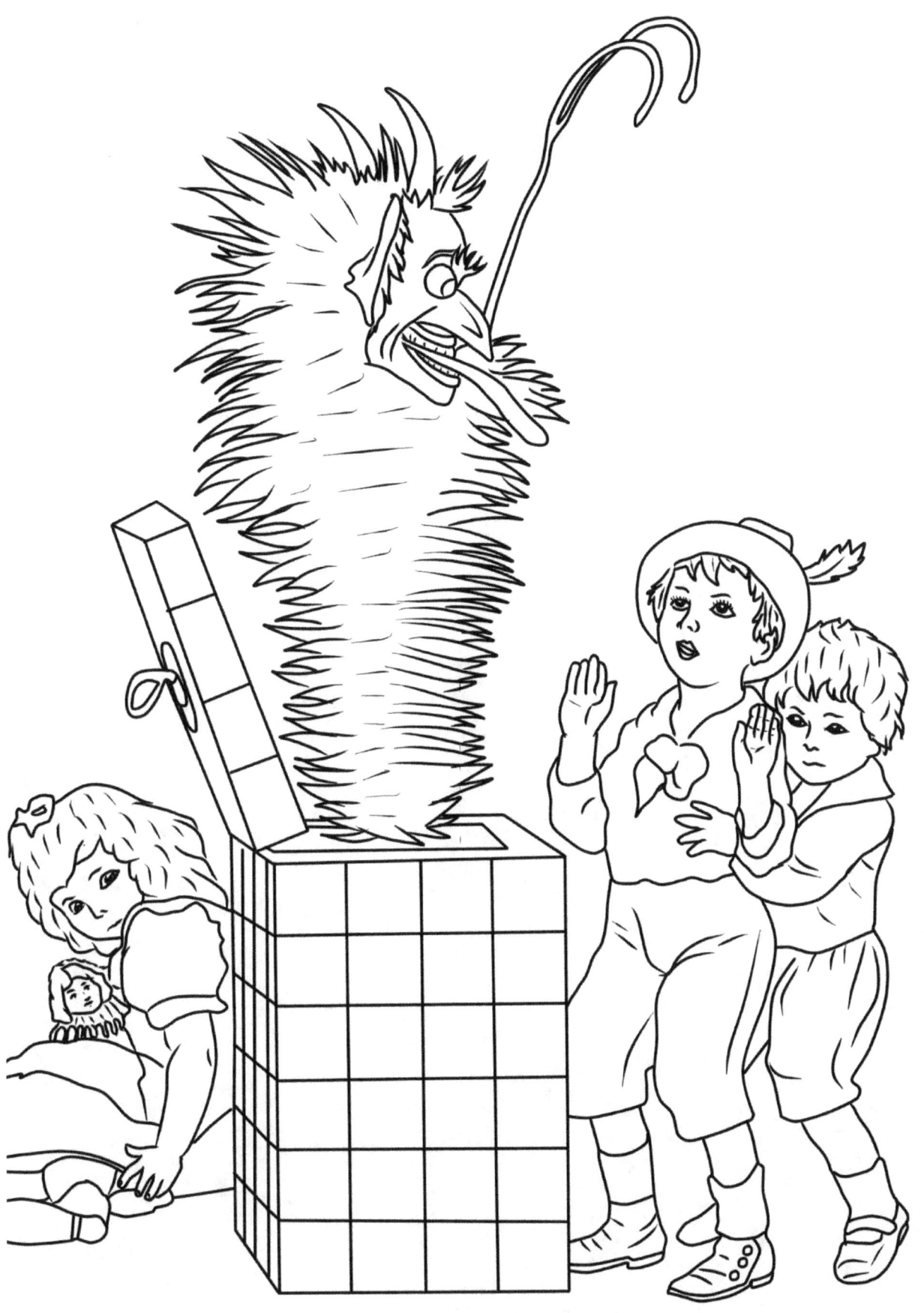

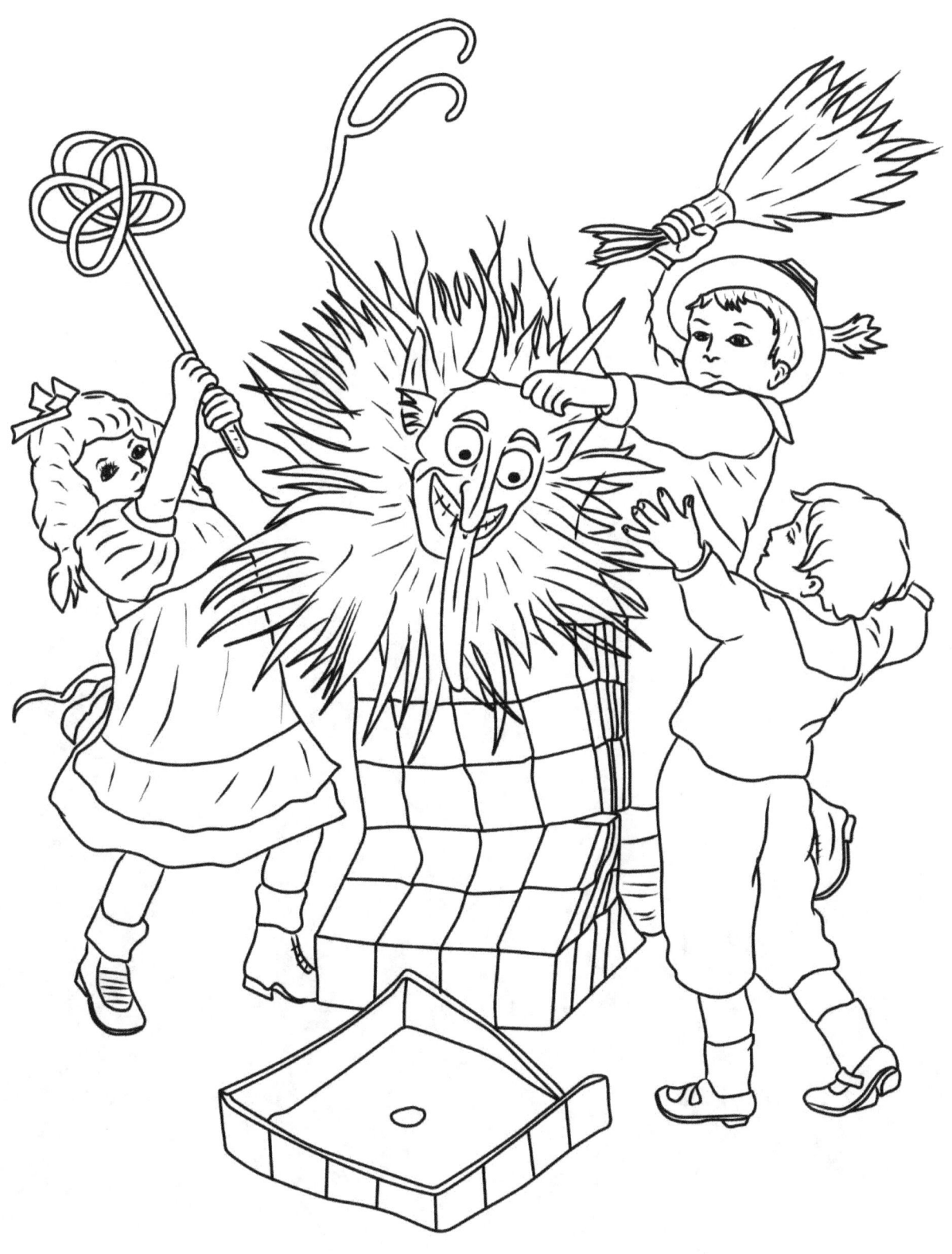

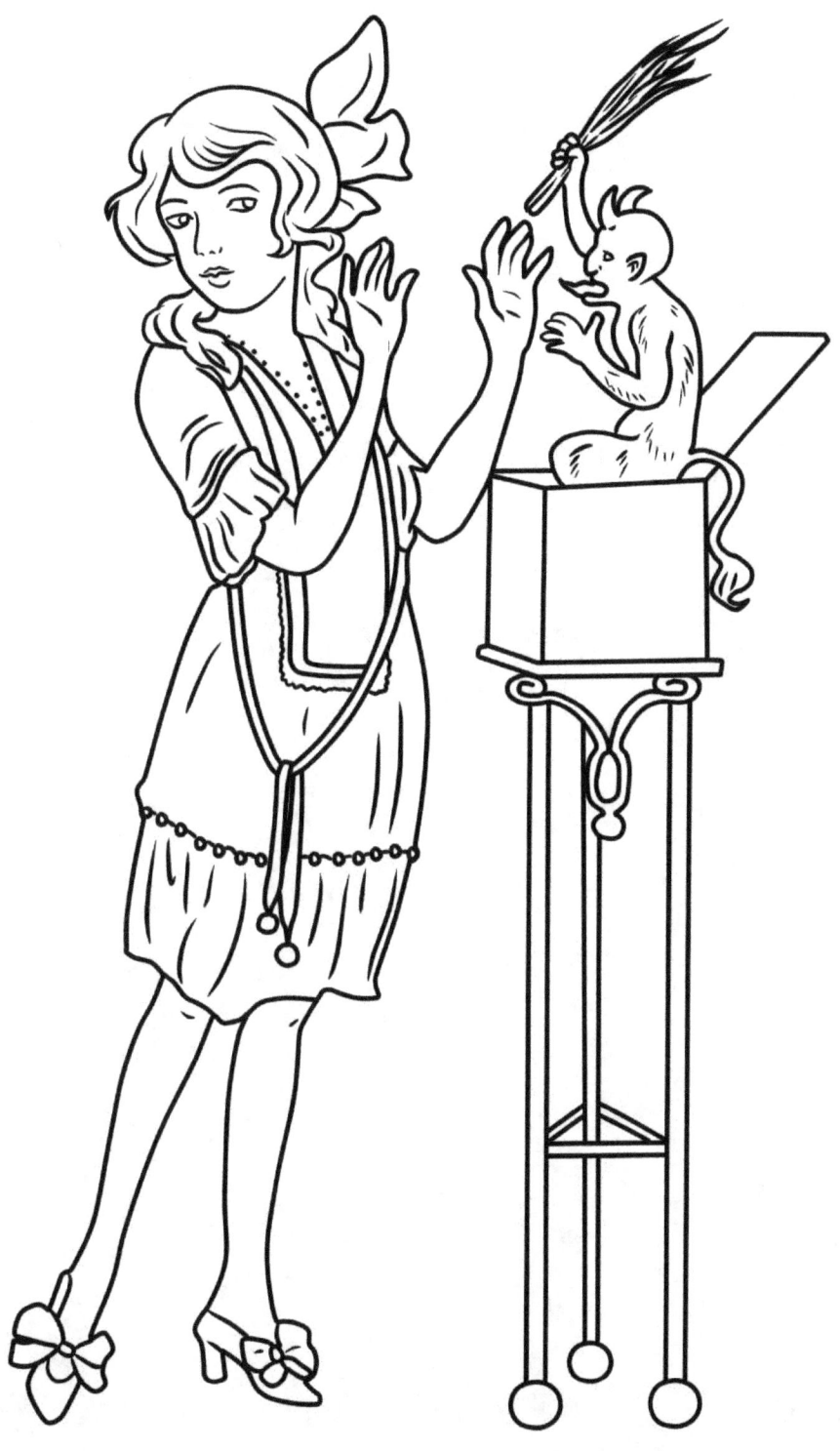

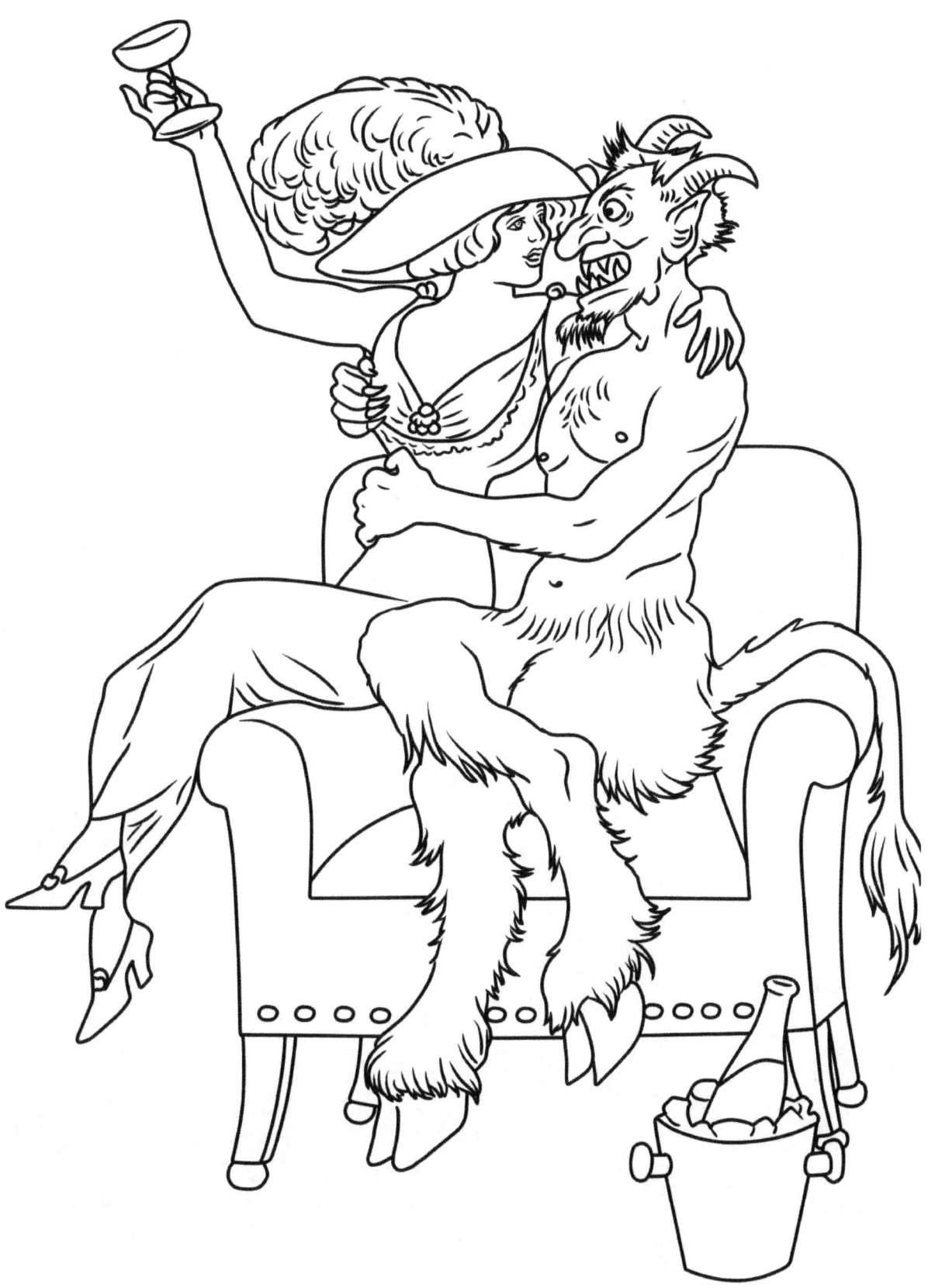

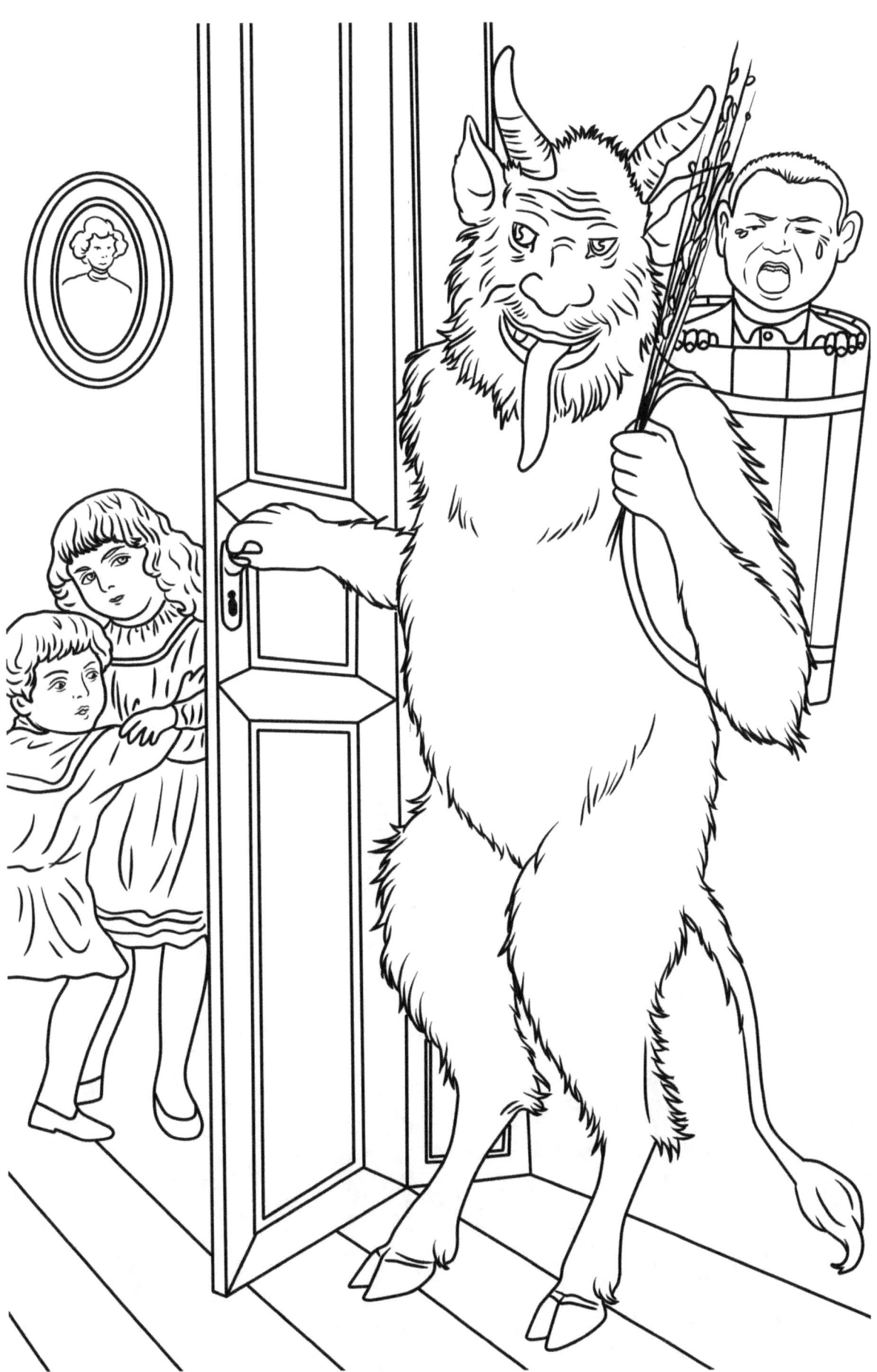

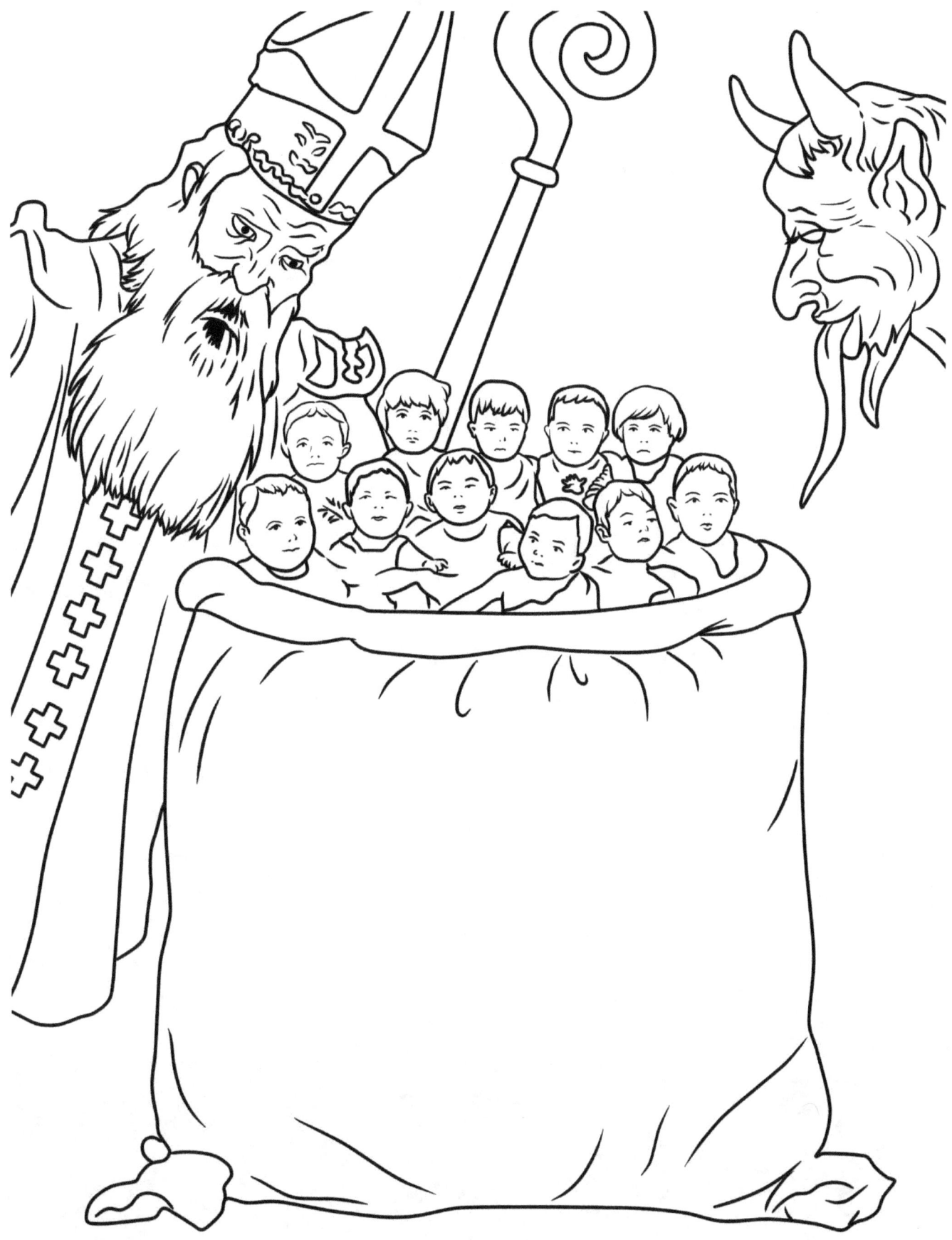

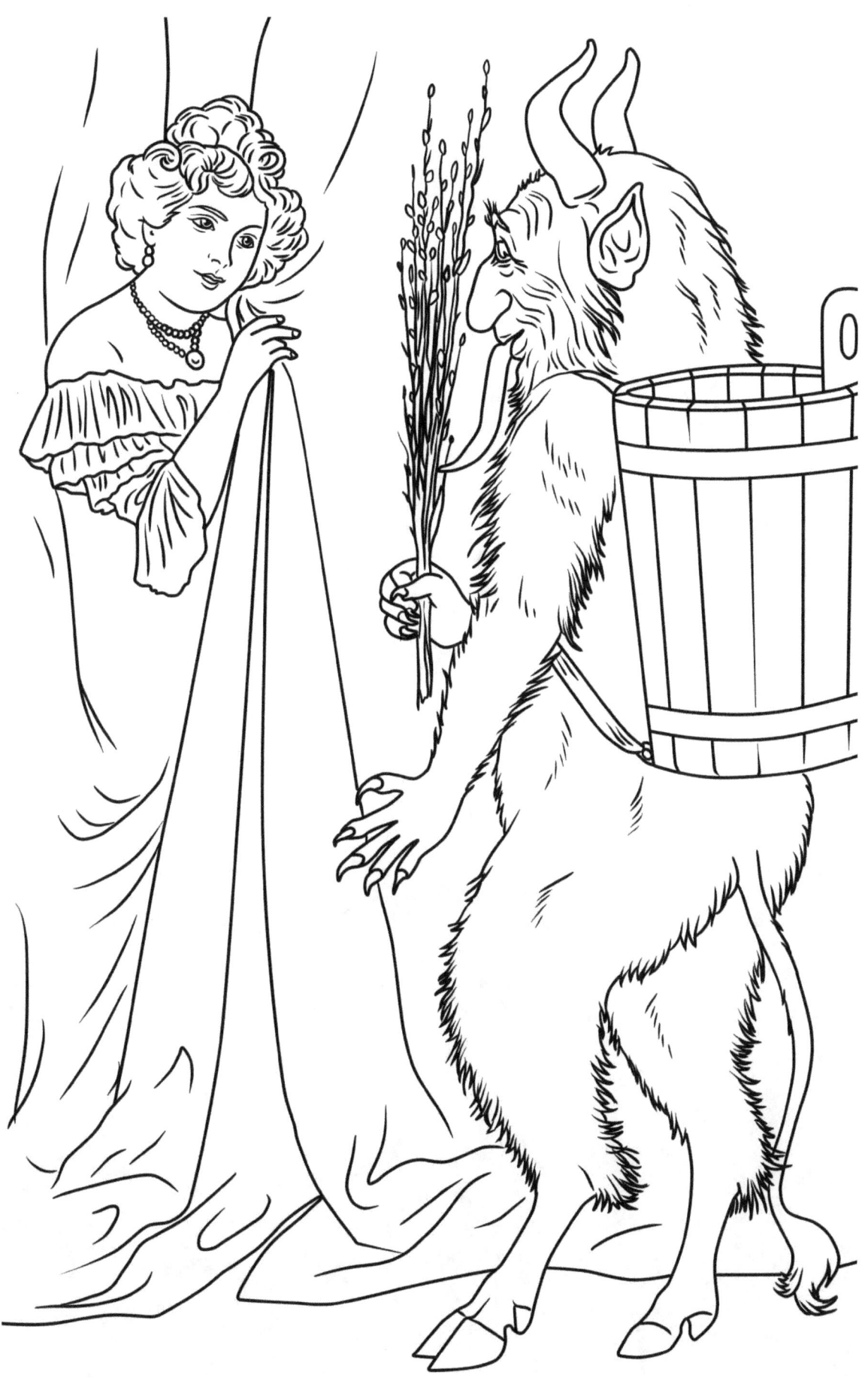

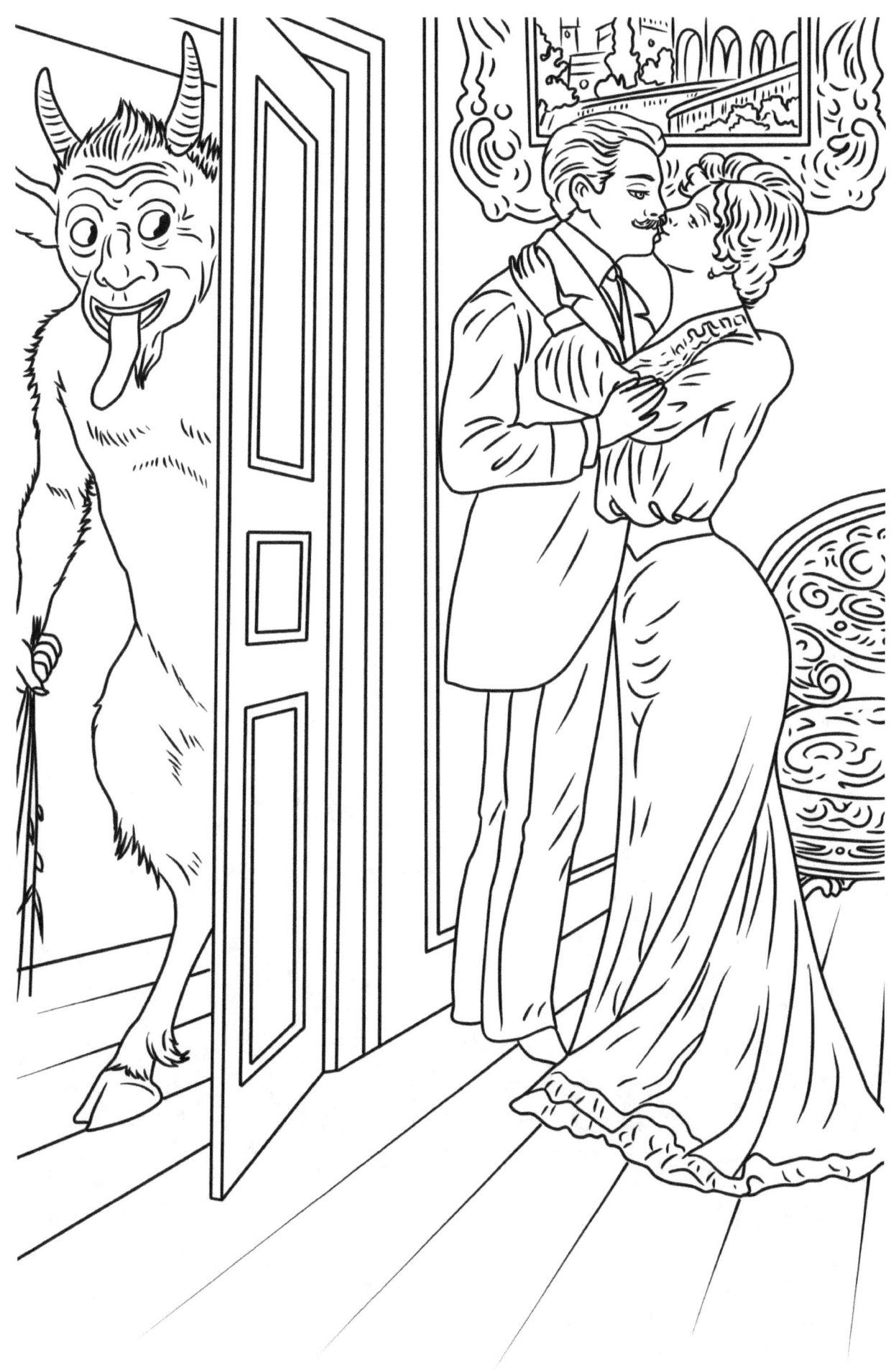

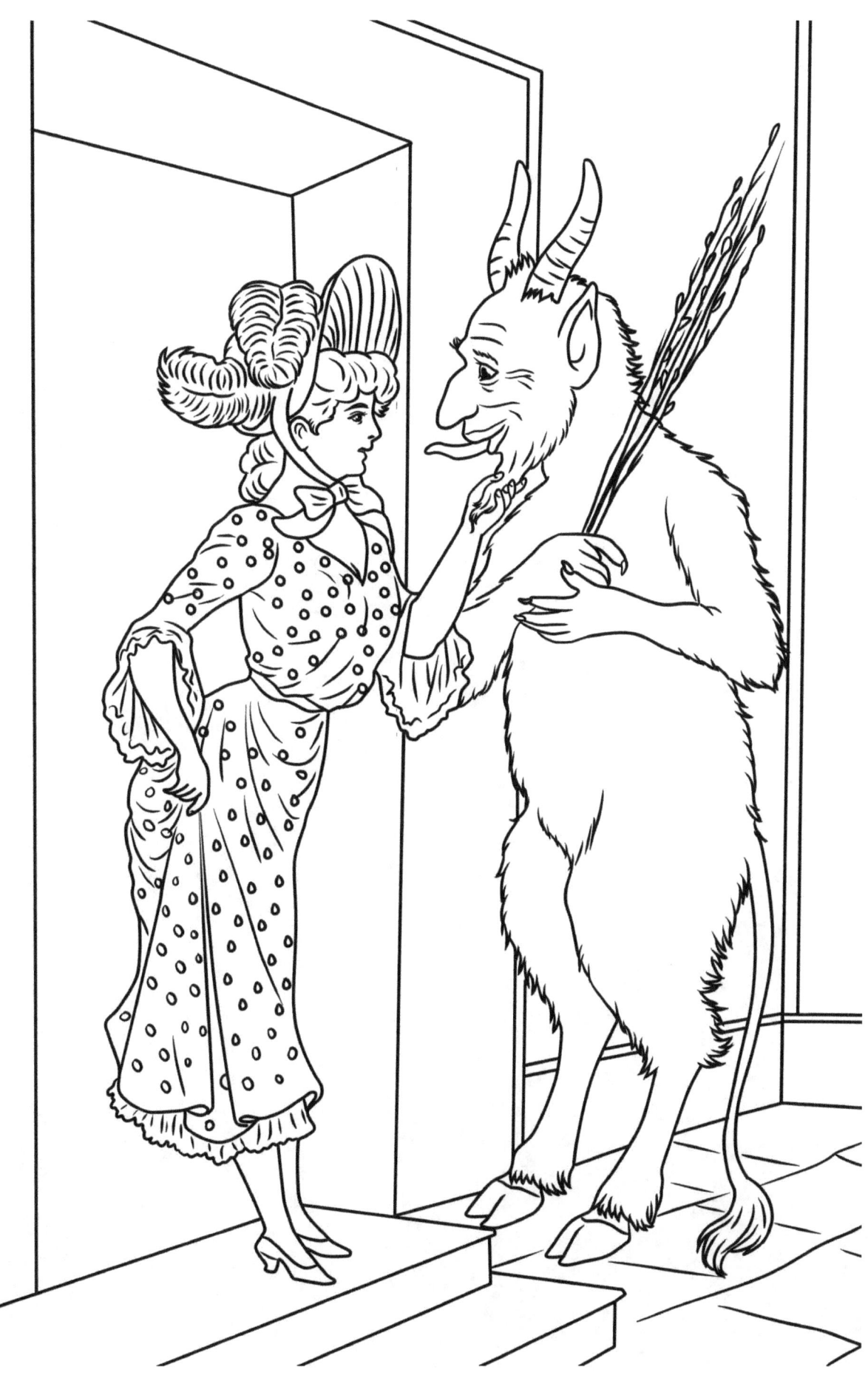

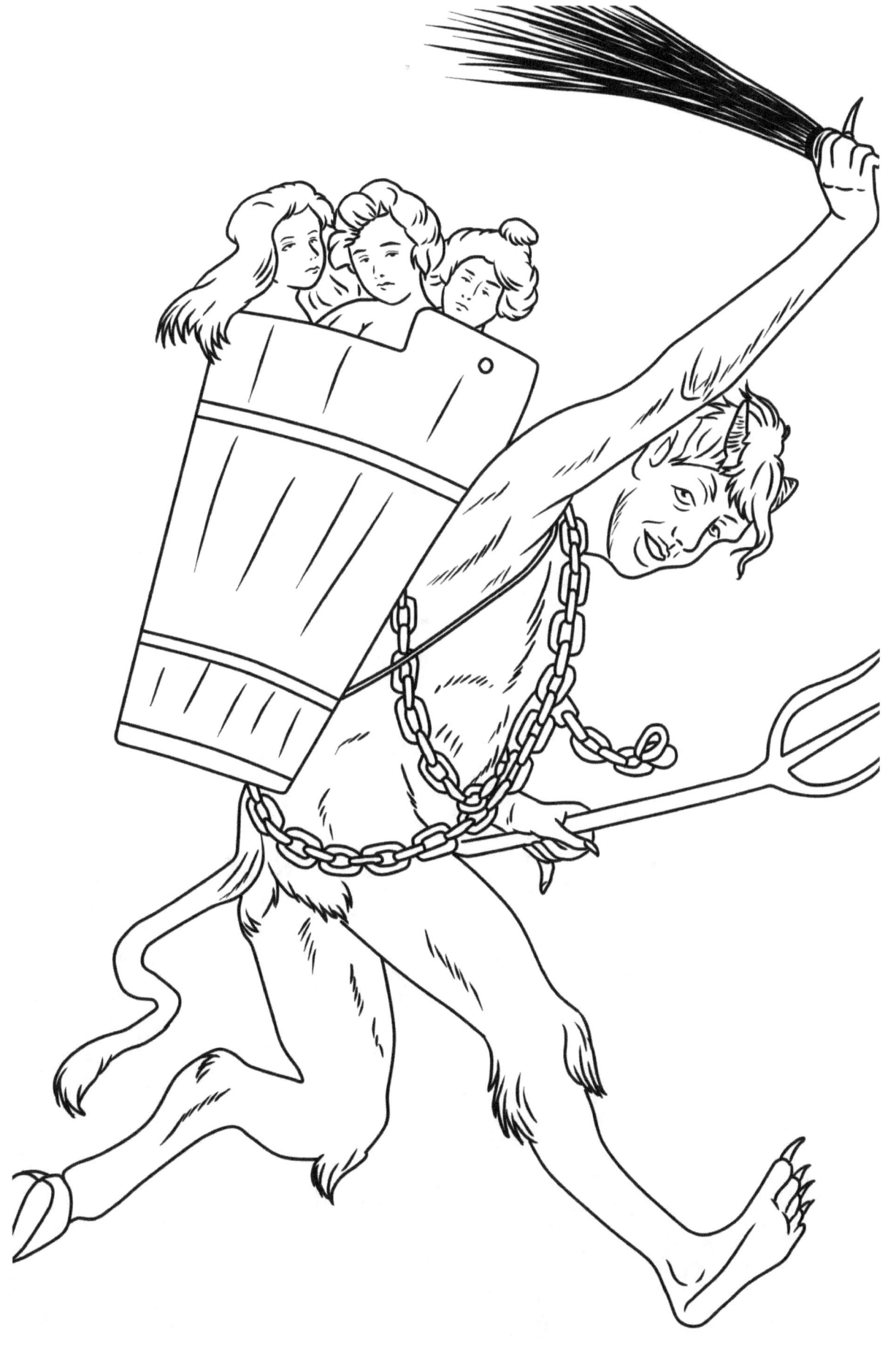

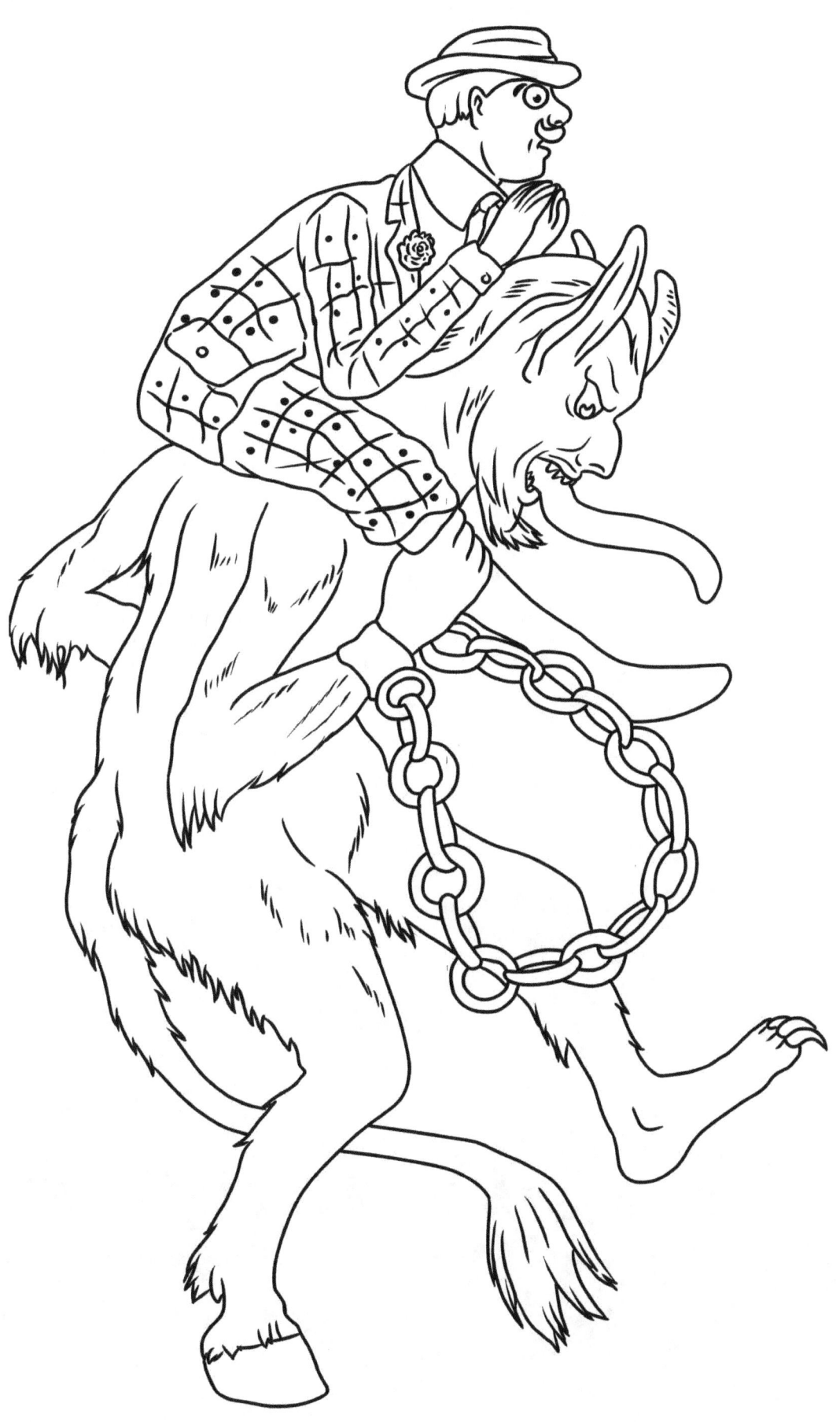

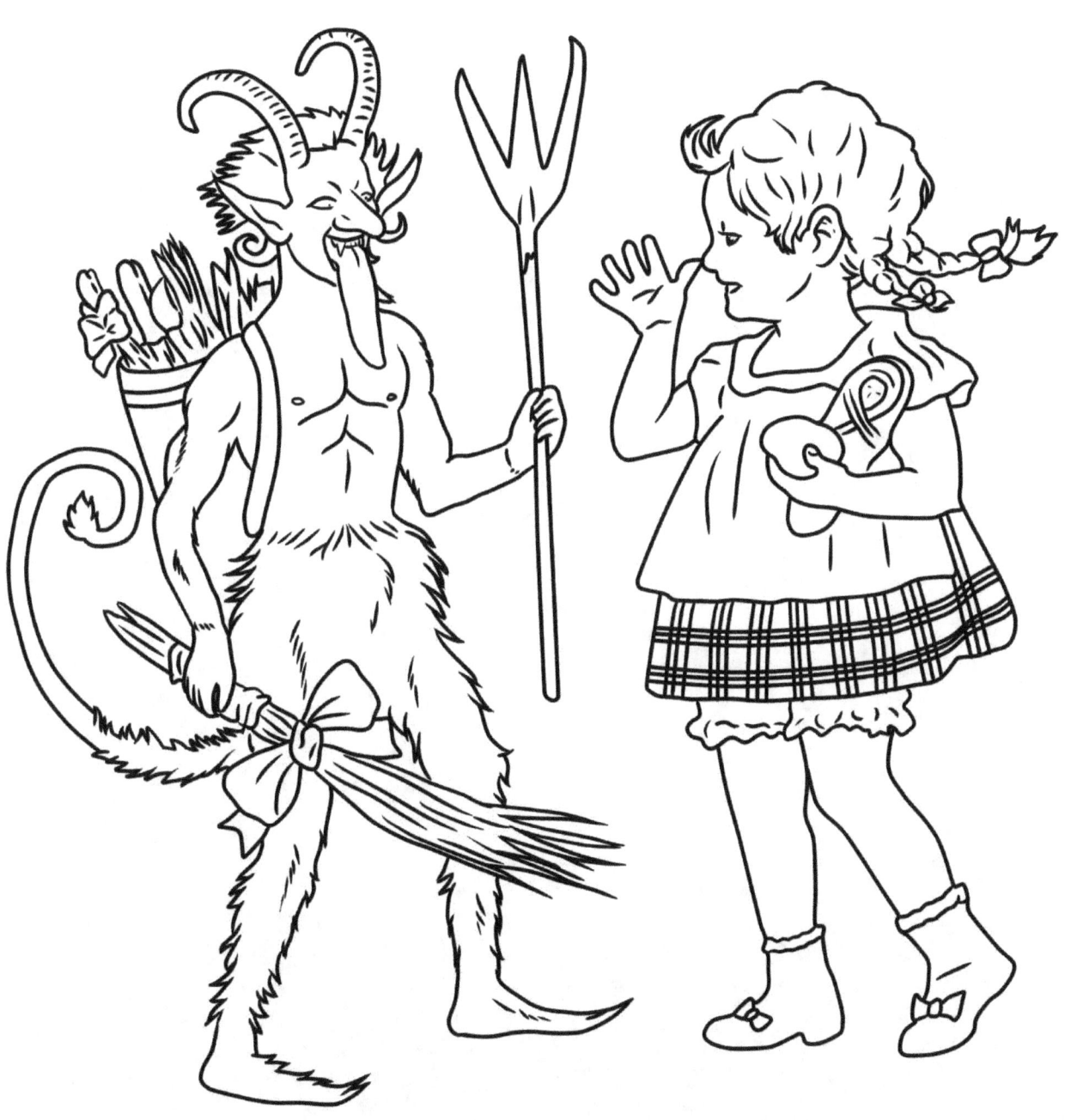

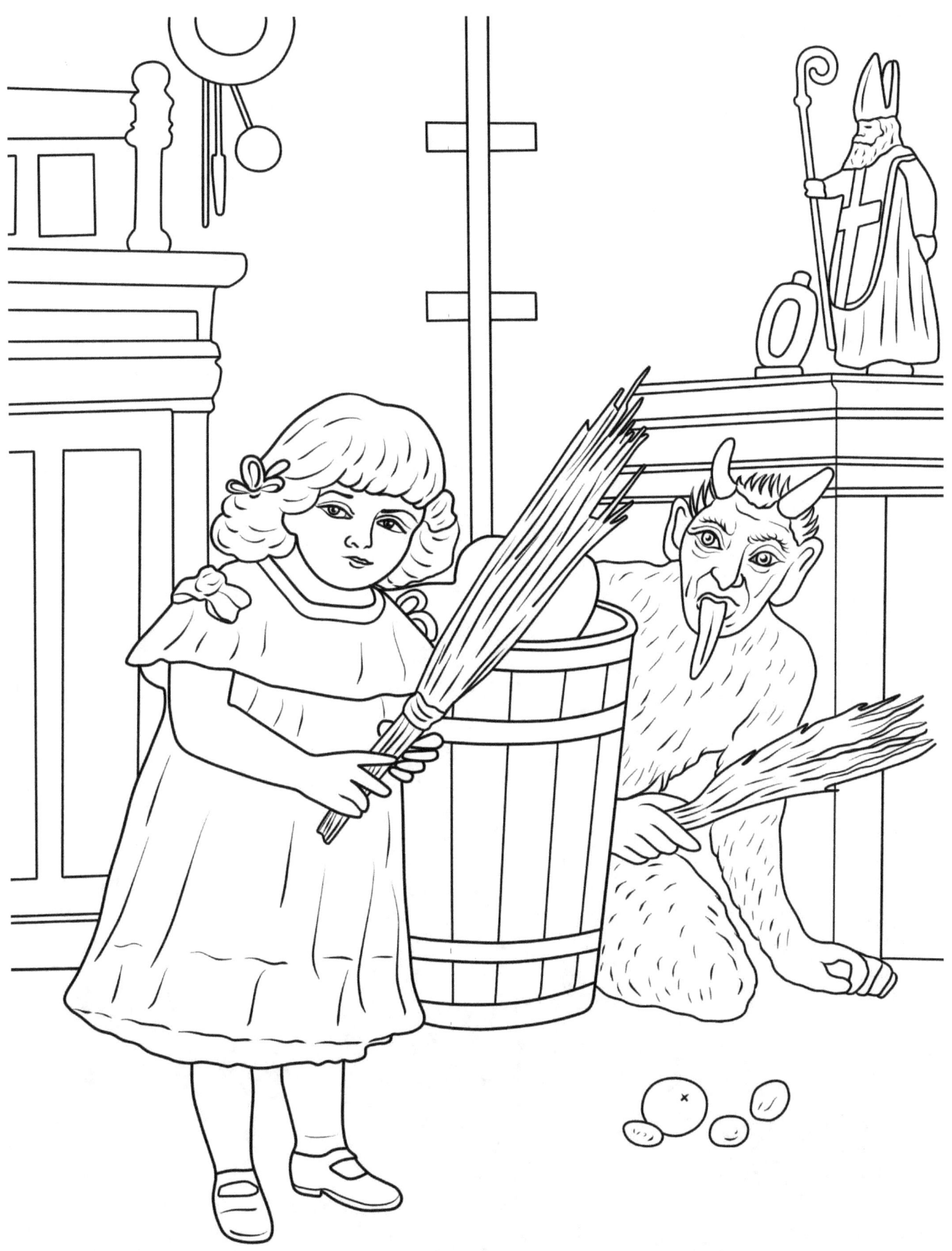

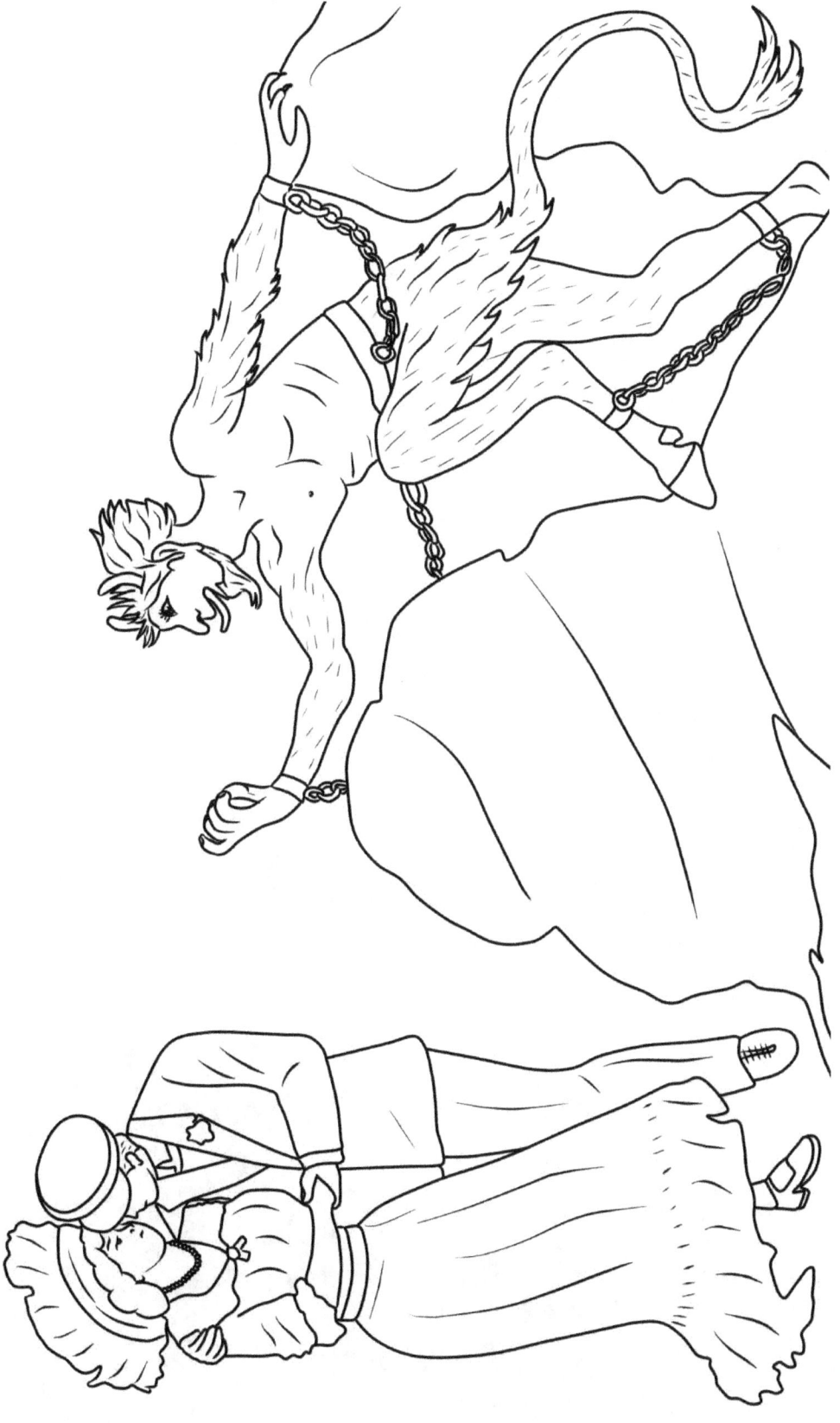

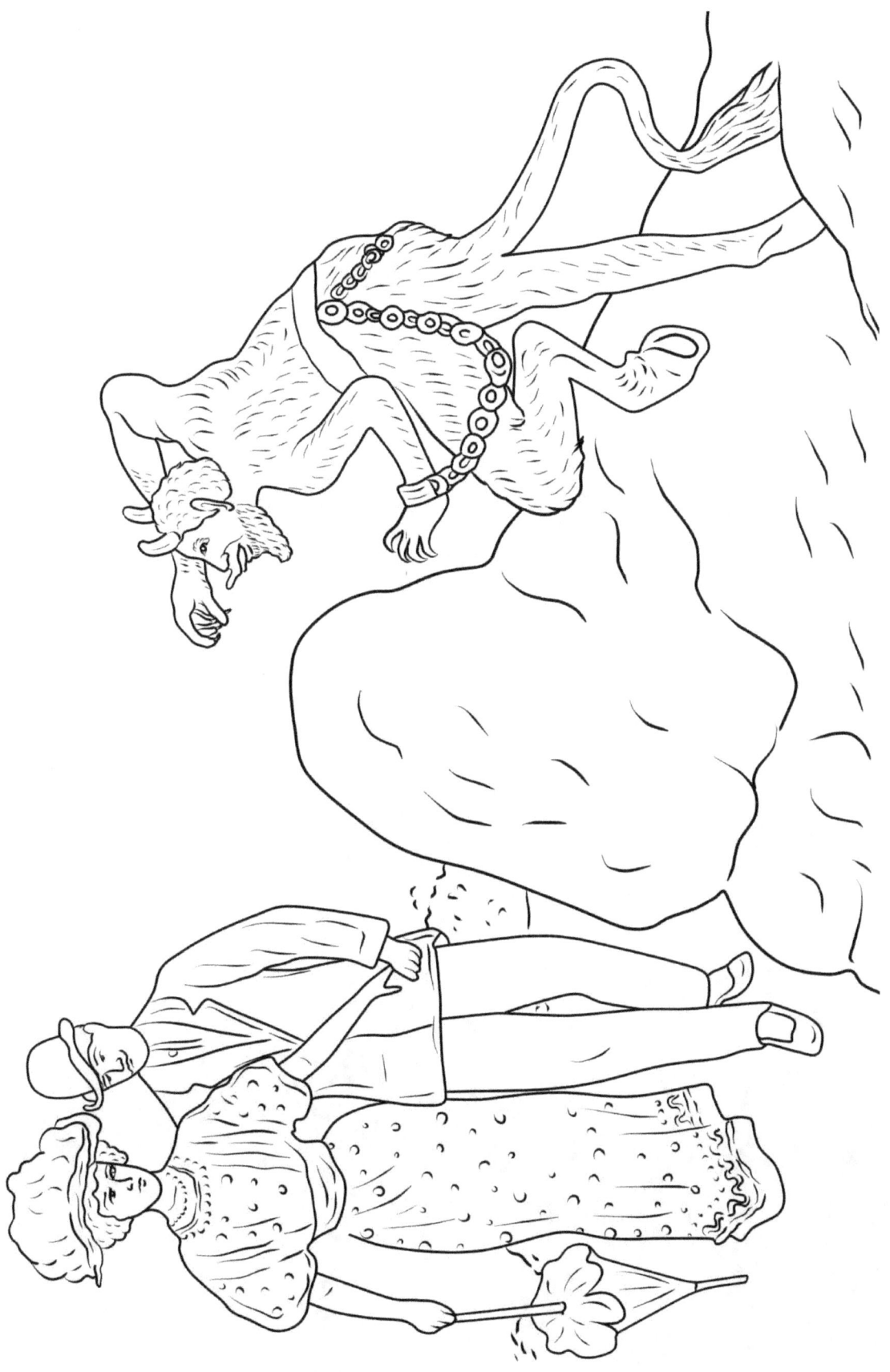

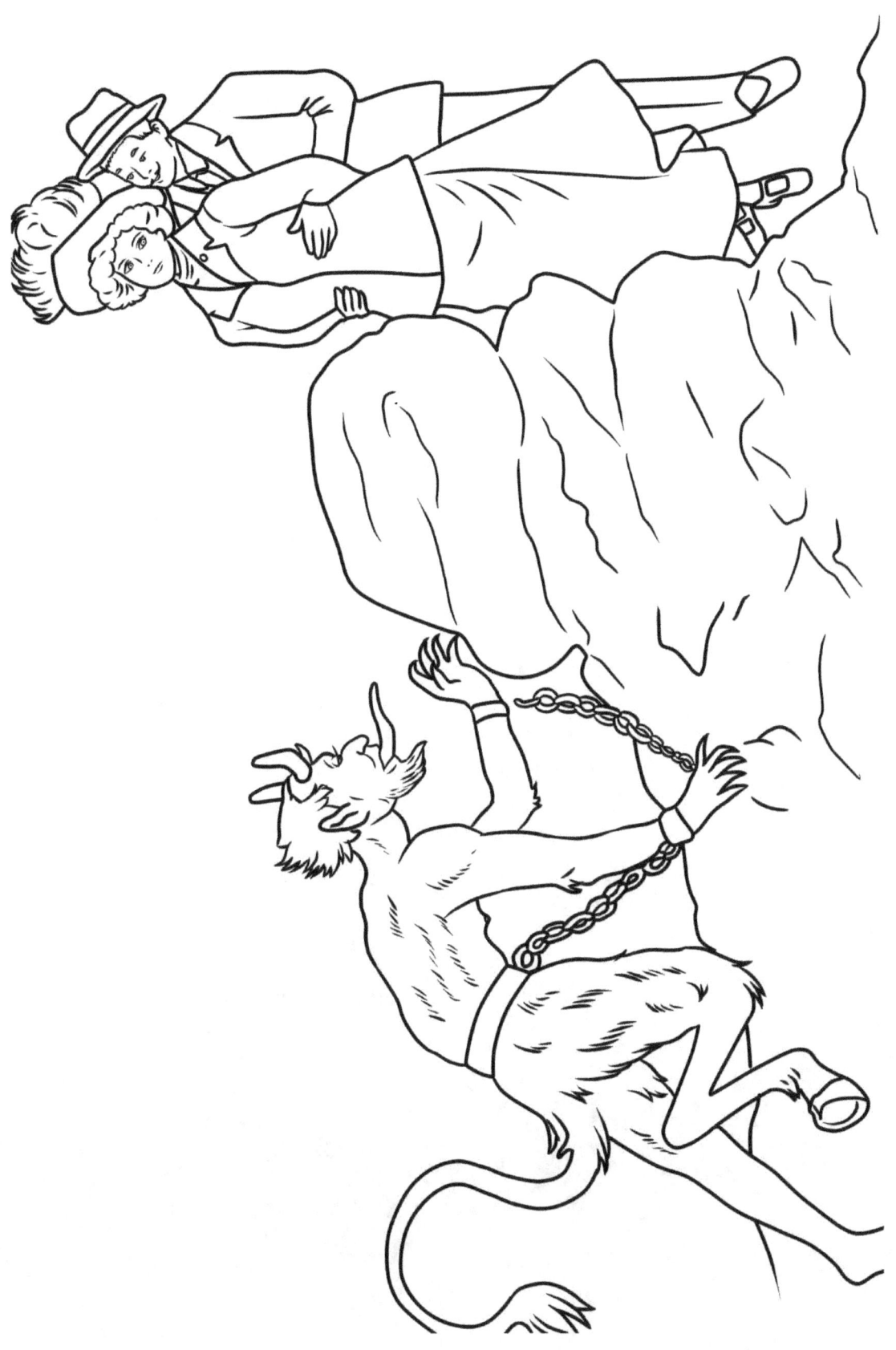

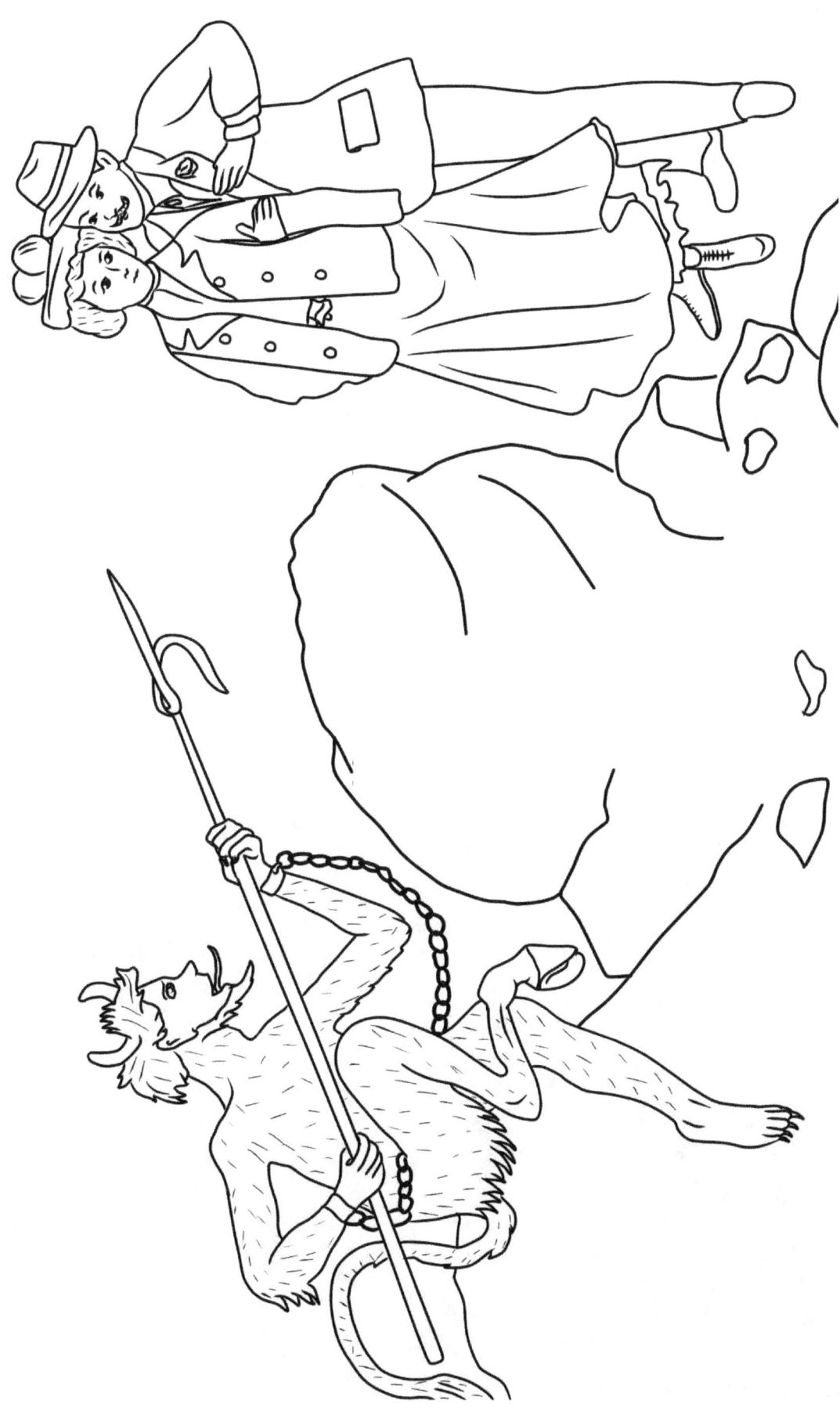

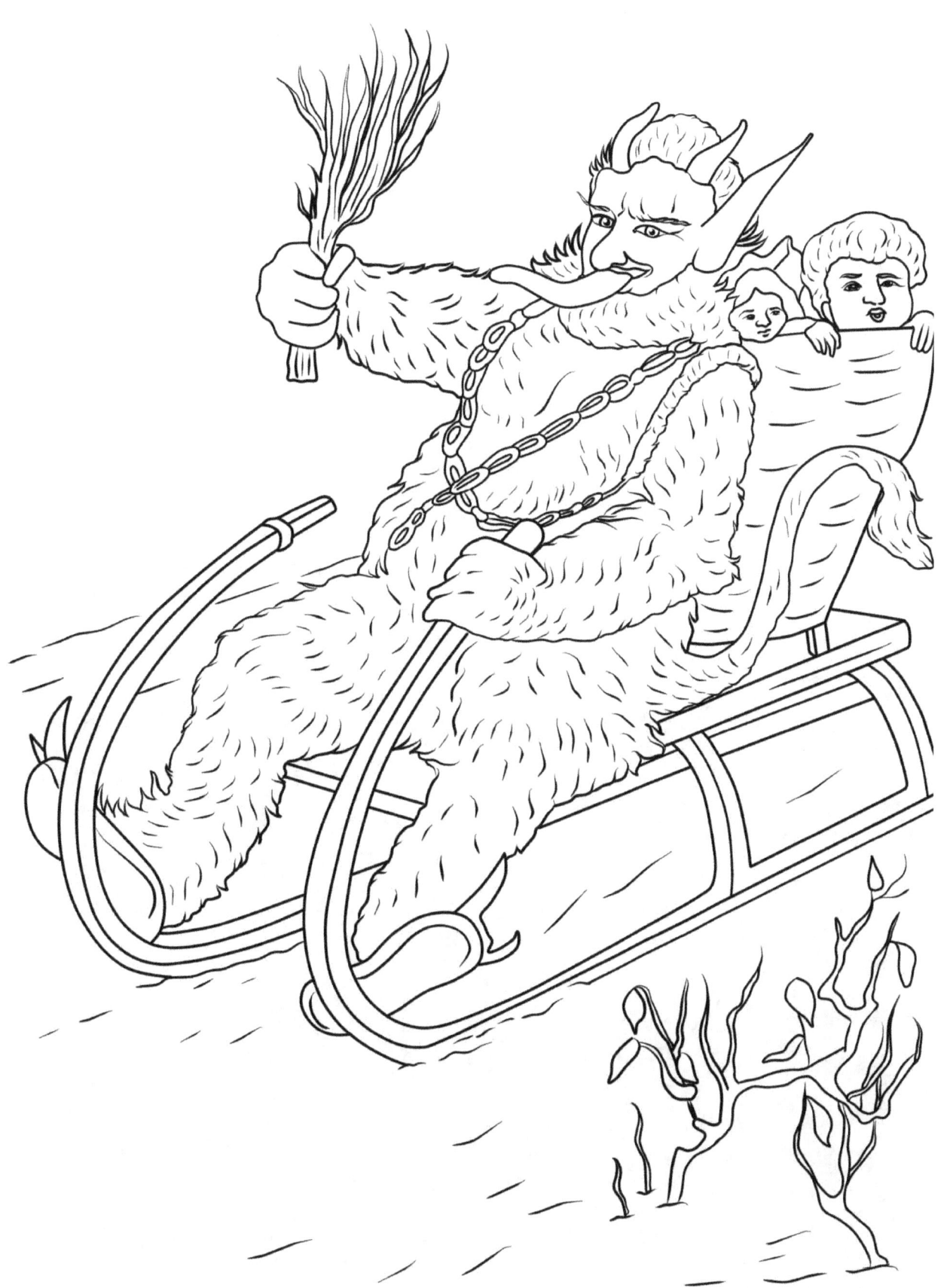

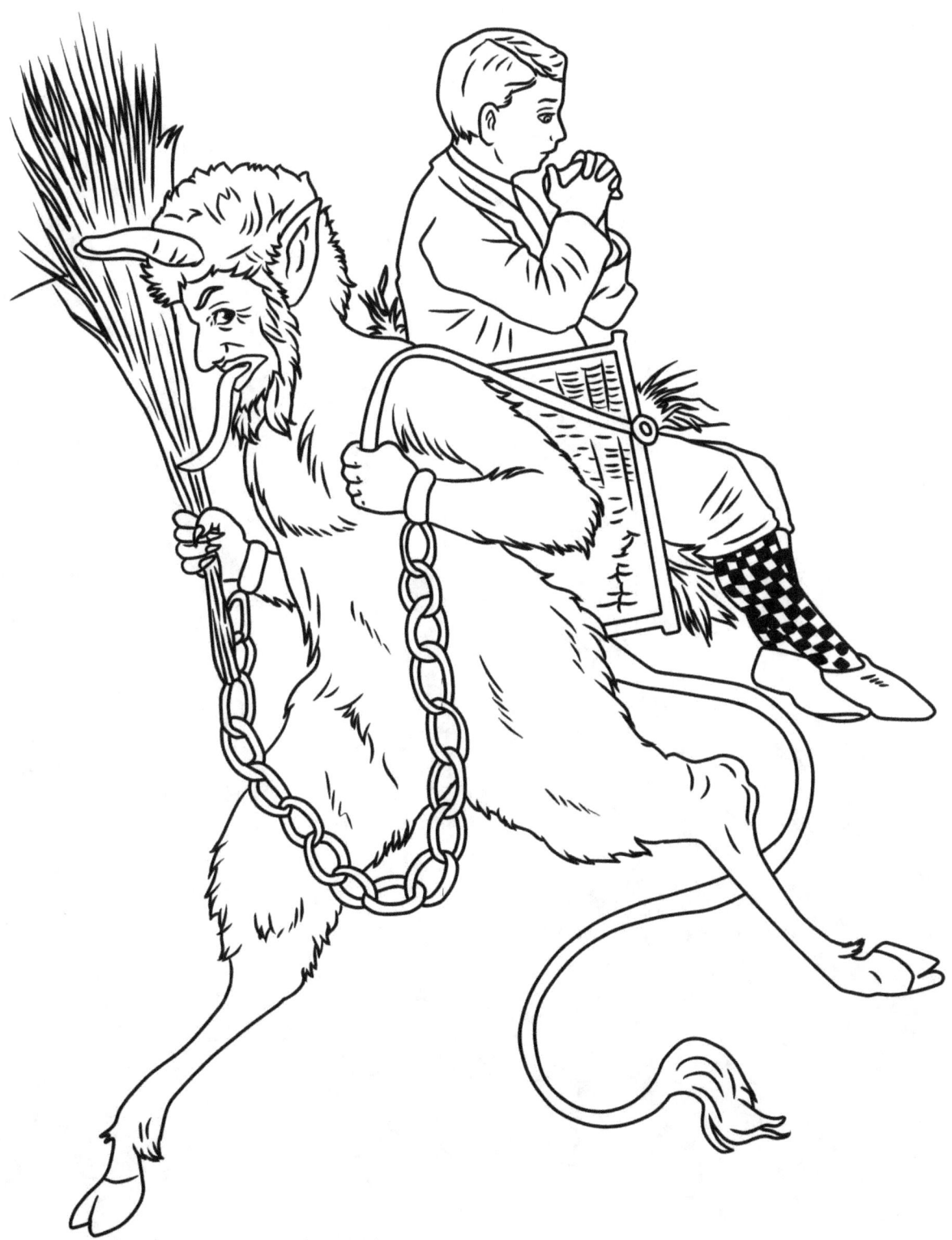

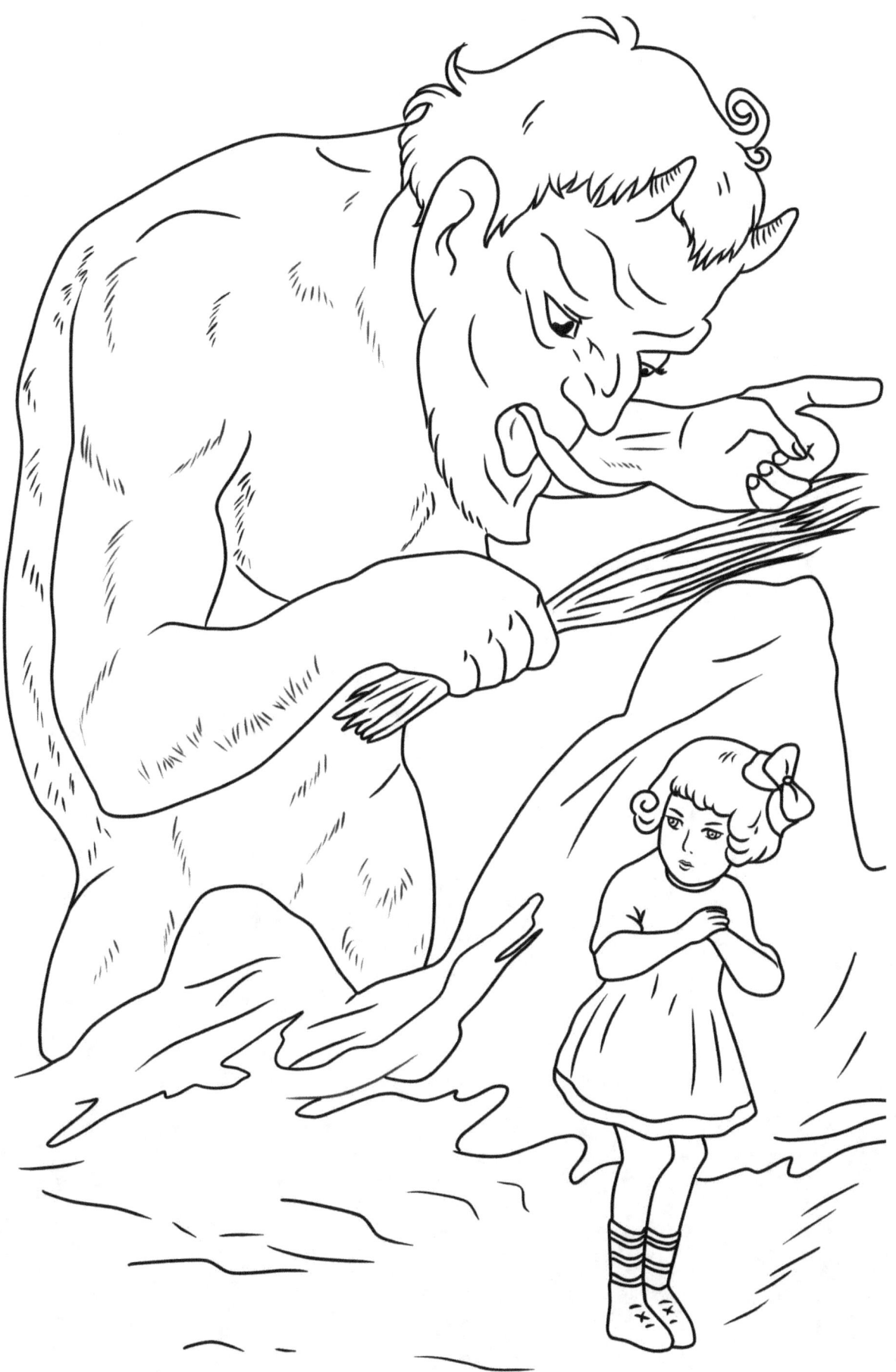

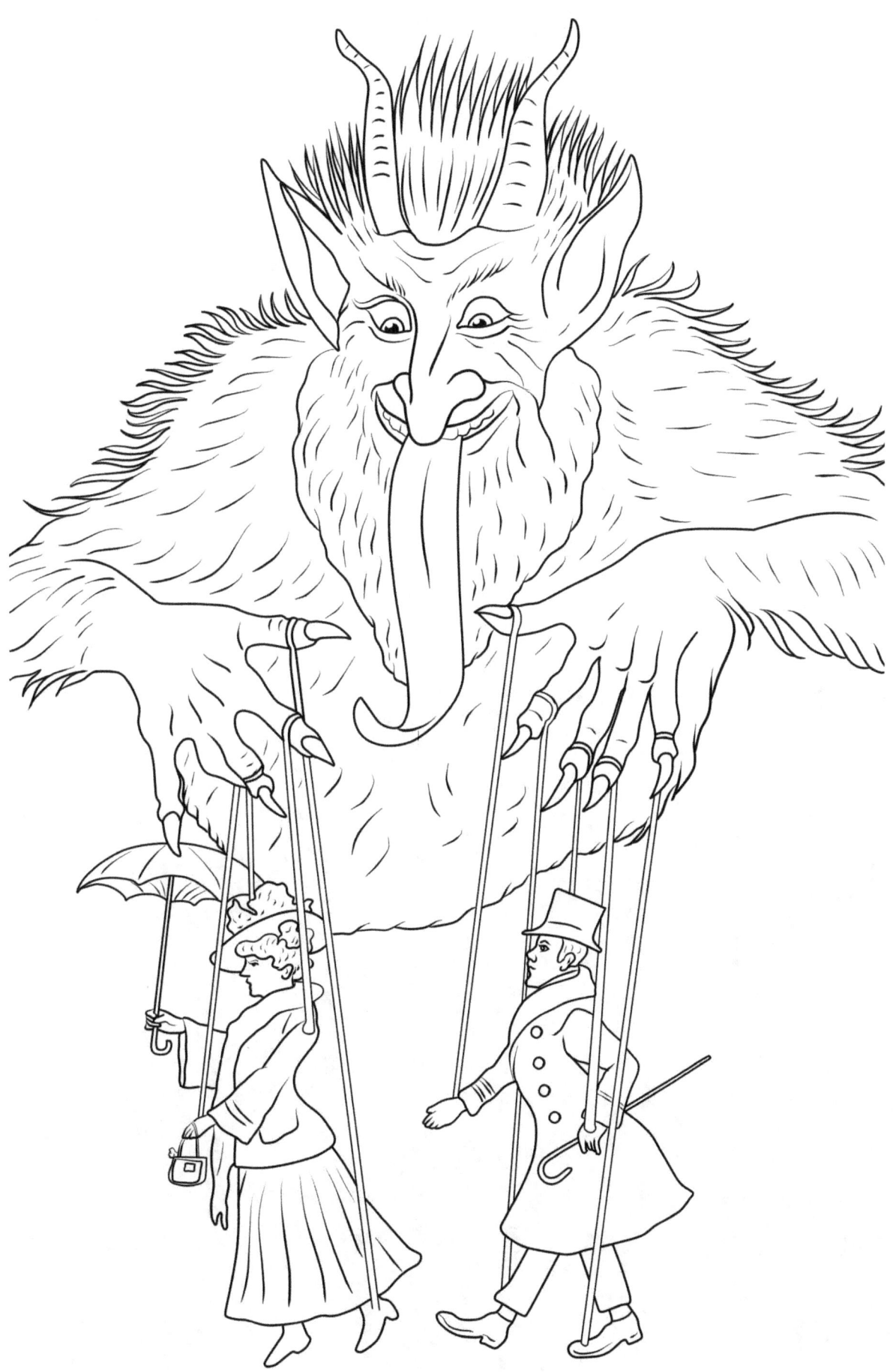

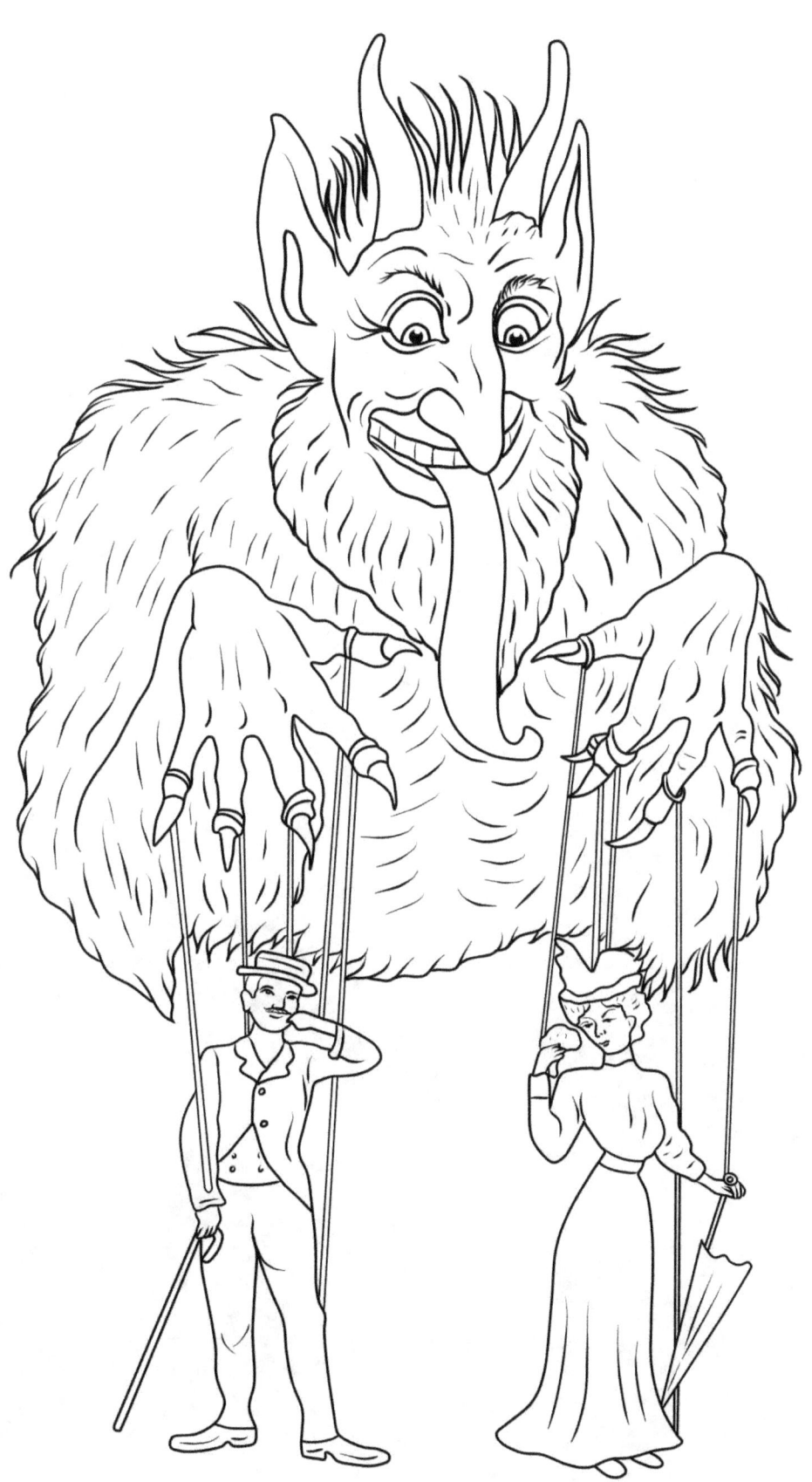

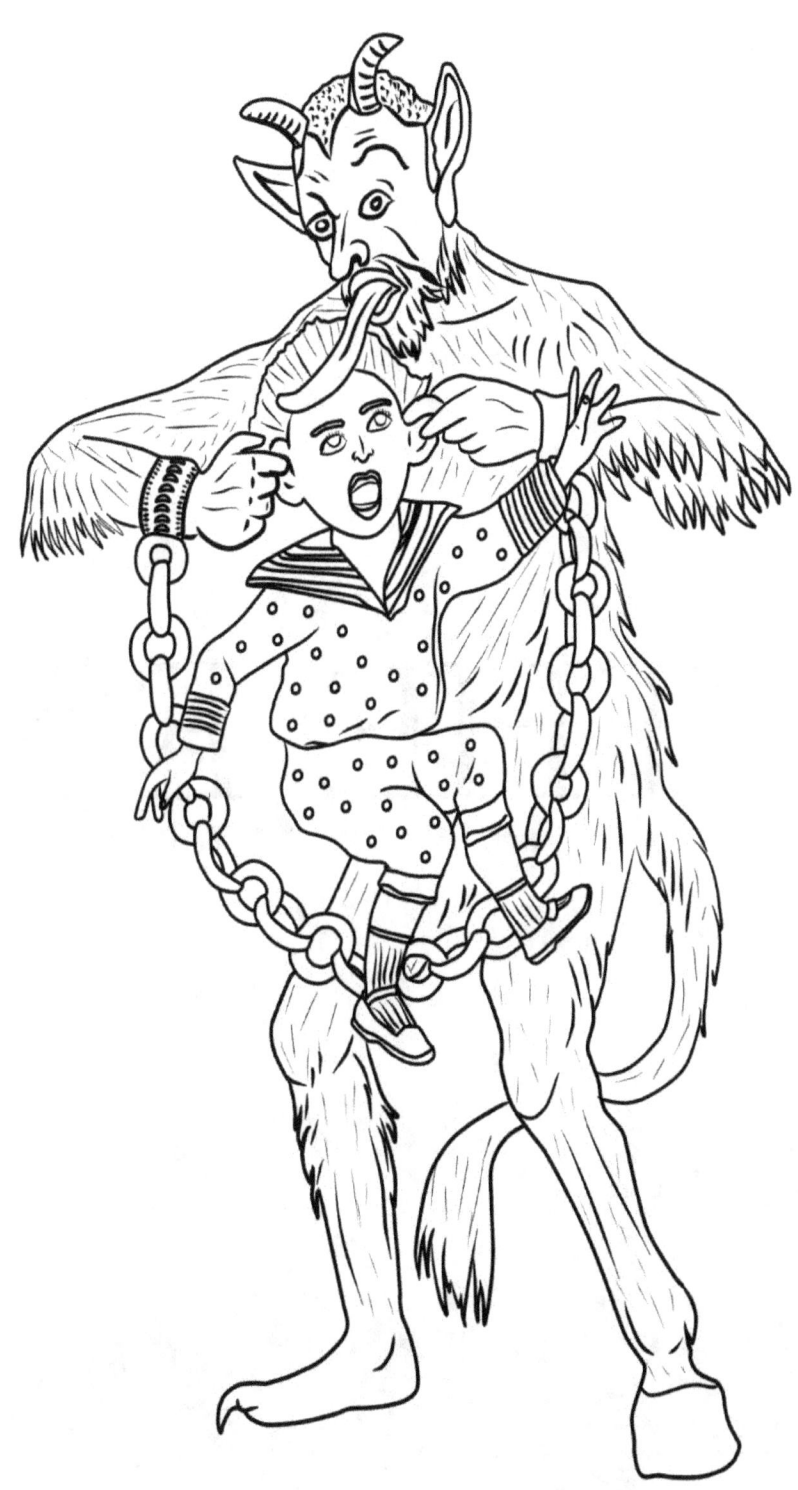

# THE END

# ABOUT THE AUTHOR

Jordan Colton has been an avid fan of horror and Halloween since he was a little boy. He grew up creating haunted houses in his basement to scare the neighborhood kids, and that passion grew into a profession as he got older. He spends his Halloween seasons scaring people in professional haunts all over Utah. He has trained hundreds of actors and staff in the nature of scaring, along with designing and building elaborate props and sets to increase the sense of fear guests have in his haunted houses. Jordan currently resides in Utah with his cat and horror film collection.